Praise for NIAGARA FALLS CONFIDENTIAL ...

"A scandalously open-and-shut guilty pleasure. It's like reading a localized version of Kenneth Anger's Hollywood Babylon."
- Artvoice, Buffalo

"Like Hemingway, Breslin ... Tough and opinionated."
- Ken Baka, Sun Newspapers, Cleveland

"A hellish postcard from the honeymoon capital."
- John Petkovic, Cleveland Plain Dealer

"Reads like a bizarre flipside to dime-a-dozen tourist books."
- John Law, Niagara Falls (Ont.) Review

"Some of the juiciest mob exposes, serial killer tales, celebrity scandal and other muck raked from the streets of the Cataract City."
- Buffalo Spree

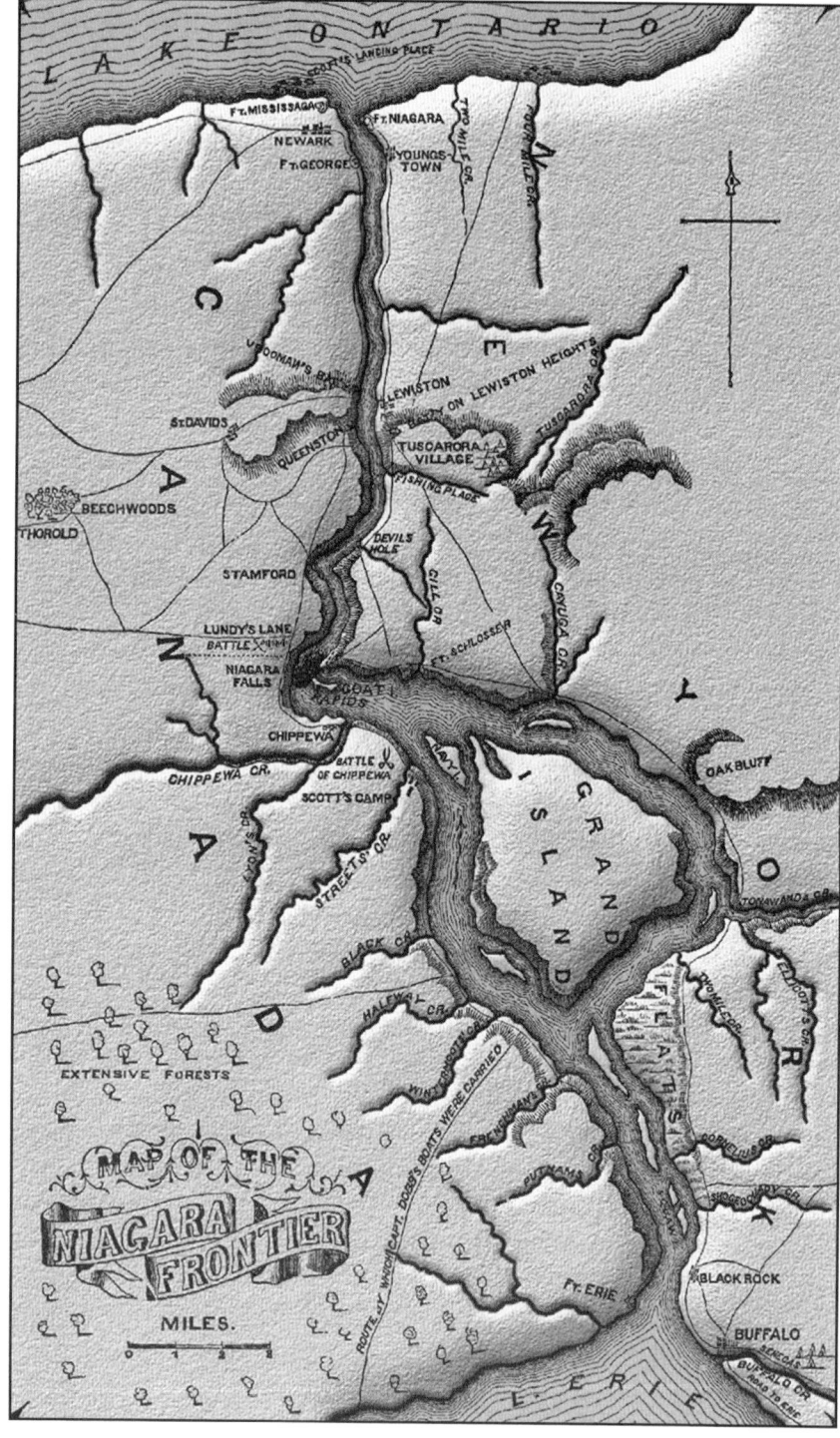

MAP OF THE NIAGARA FRONTIER

MILES.

NIAGARA FALLS CONFIDENTIAL

Newly Revised & Expanded

Edited by Mike & Rebecca Hudson

POWER CITY PRESS

Niagara Falls Confidential

Second Edition, Revised & Expanded

ISBN 978-0-615-29642-5

Printed in the United States by Dual Printing

COVER DESIGN: Margaret Coghlan

Power City Press
1625 Buffalo Ave.
Suite 2A
Niagara Falls, N.Y. 14303

E-mail: pagan@sysr.com

TABLE OF CONTENTS

"The Niagara Falls is simply a vast amount of water going the wrong way over some unnecessary rocks; the sight of that waterfall must be one of the earliest and keenest disappointments in American married life."

Oscar Wilde, 1882

"I gave the name of Jack Drake, but when they searched me they found letters addressed to Jack London. This caused trouble and required explanation, all of which has passed from my mind, and to this day I do not know whether I was pinched as Jack Drake or Jack London. But one or the other, it should be there today in the prison register of Niagara Falls."

Jack London, 1907

MOMMY'S LITTLE BATMAN

By Mike Hudson

Det. Frank Coney is something of a legend in Western New York law enforcement circles, having cracked countless tough cases in his nearly 40 years of investigating homicides and other major crimes in the tourist mecca of Niagara Falls.

But nothing he had seen prepared him for the gruesome carnage that met his eyes early on the morning of June 25, 1988. The grisly scene inside the neat and modest brick home in the city's LaSalle section turned even Coney's cast-iron stomach.

In a narrow hallway upstairs he found the body of a woman. The first cops on the scene thought she'd been decapitated, but her head hadn't been cut off so much as beaten to pieces. Blood and gore dripped from the walls and ceiling, spilling through the bedroom doorway on either side. One of the dead woman's fingers lay several feet away, apparently knocked off as she raised her hand to defend herself from a vicious blow. Nearby was the murder weapon, a baseball bat drenched in blood, with bits of skull and skin adhering to its barrel.

The corpse was that of Marge Shrubsall, a 56-year-old widow and single mother. Her clean-cut 17-year-old son Billy, the prime suspect in the brutal slaying, sat on a couch downstairs.

Wearing a torn and bloody T-shirt and jeans, the kid had already given police two different accounts of his mother's murder. In the first, Billy Shrubsall spun a yarn about two masked intruders who broke in while he was away and viciously attacked the woman. In the second, he told a tale of child abuse and parental dysfunction on a horrific scale. He had killed his mother himself, he said, in self-defense.

"She says, 'I'll kill you, ya SOB,' and I — I just turned and reached for the first thing and I hit her," he said. "I hit her the first time, the first few times or whatever, so many times, out of fear, and then after that, I don't know."

Later at the police station, the athletic six-footer ate a hero sandwich as his 15-year-old girlfriend sat sobbing beside him.

"Calm down," he said without looking at her. "This is no big thing."

Billy Shrubsall was still wearing the blood-spattered T-shirt. Coney said the young killer's primary concern was the commencement address he was scheduled to deliver later that afternoon as valedictorian of his high school class.

Police had found a handwritten copy of the speech at the Shrubsall home, shortly after Marge's battered body was bagged and tagged and taken to the morgue.

"On a personal note, I would like to thank my mother, who taught me my reach should exceed my grasp," it ended. "Thank you, Mom."

The police questioning continued throughout the day, and Billy's justification for committing one of the most heinous crimes known to man became more and more detailed.

"It's no small threat that she could kill with her bare hands 'cause she's much stronger than I am," he told the cops. "I'm just a 17-year-old kid, you know. I mean she's ... she's ... she puts fear in me, and her anger makes it all the worse."

When asked why he first said Marge was killed by intruders, Shrubsall stunned investigators by saying he was trying to protect his family's good reputation.

"I didn't want that to happen to her name, and I didn't want it to happen to my name. And, you know, I just didn't want it to happen," he said.

Coney said he had never seen a cooler customer under interrogation.

"For a kid whose mother had just been brutally killed, he showed no emotion at all," Coney said. "He was working on ways to take the system for a ride right from the start."

In his statement to police, Billy said he'd returned home from his girlfriend's house shortly before his midnight curfew to find his mother asleep in bed. His girlfriend then called to say he'd left his watch and some photographs behind, and he returned to get them.

When he got home the second time, at around 1 a.m., Marge Shrubsall was sitting in her car in the driveway, looking furious and about to go out looking for him.

She began screaming insanely, the young killer said.

"You slime! Your girlfriend's a whore! Her family are perverts!" Billy told the cops she ranted.

She made him clean the house, hurling insults all along, he said. Finally, at 3 a.m., she picked up the phone and said she was calling his girlfriend's parents to "tell them their daughter's a slut." Billy said that when he attempted to hang the phone up she beat him, first with the receiver and then with her elbows and fists. She said she would kill him, he said.

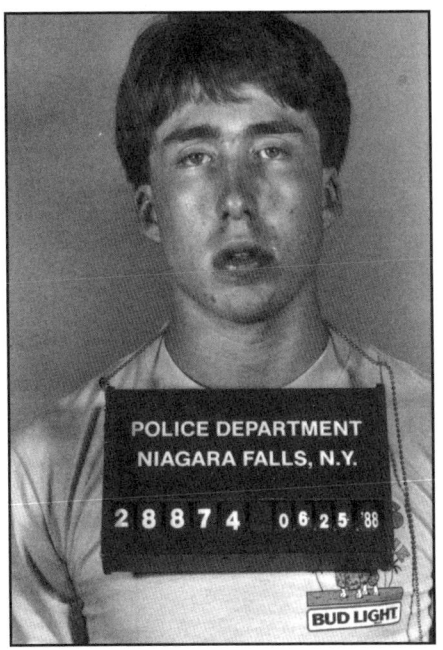

'MISUNDERSTOOD'? Niagara Falls Police took Billy Shrubsall's mugshot after the horrifying baseball-bat murder of his mother.

Coney wasn't buying any of it. The little bastard had smashed his mother's head to pieces with 20 blows of a 40-ounce Louisville Slugger, delivering at least 15 of them after she'd gone down and couldn't possibly have posed any threat.

"He was a murderer, not a mixed-up kid," the veteran detective said.

After giving his statement, Billy Shrubsall was booked on charges of second-degree murder and weapons possession. His savage act of matricide seemed like an open-and-shut case.

But Billy was no ordinary killer. He wasn't even an ordinary mother-killer. Like Michael Myers in the Halloween movies, he would return again and again, striking terror into the hearts of his victims.

It was no time at all before a veritable Greek chorus of the usual bleeding-heart suspects was lined up at the jailhouse door, offering to defend Billy and even portraying him as the victim in the case.

There was Paul Cleary, an attorney best known for winning the acquittal of an allegedly battered wife who shot her husband to death.

"Nobody portrays Billy Shrubsall as an altar boy, but in 24 hours the kid went from being the smart kid, No. 1 in his class, to being Jack the Ripper," he said. "I think that image has survived and I wonder what effect it's having on this case."

Cleary enlisted the aid of Dr. Charles Patrick Ewing, a forensic psychologist from the University of Buffalo, whose pet theory held that no child would kill his parent unless he was the victim of horrible abuse.

Ewing said Marge Shrubsall's relationship with Billy was "pathological." He characterized the dead woman, who had spent the day before her murder preparing food for her son's graduation party, as an abusive harpy.

He based all this on a four-and-a-half-hour interview he later used in preparing a book. At Shrubsall's trial, Ewing would flatly testify Billy posed no menace to society.

"The typical justification for jail time is just not there," he said. "He's not going to go out and hurt anybody."

"Is he a killer? Absolutely not. I believe he acted in self-defense, as the law defines it," Ewing added.

This sickening stew received some added seasoning from the local papers. In one article, the "300-pound" Marge Shrubsall was "ranting" and "charging" and "bellowing a torrent of obscenities" at her terrified son.

"Her unrelenting insults hurled like balls of mud," the turgid prose continued. "The fleshy fist of the hulking woman hit like a cannonball."

Poor Billy had little choice but to bash his mother's head in, the article concluded.

"In an uncontrolled rage she attacks again. ... She steamrolls after him, cornering him in his bedroom."

Such was the treatment the murdered woman received. Billy must have laughed as he sat in his jail cell and read it.

Lost in the psychobabble was the recollection of one neighbor, who saw the boy leaving the house on the afternoon before the slaying.

"Marge was watering some plants with a garden hose and, when Billy came by, she playfully squirted him," the neighbor said. "He darted away, and they both laughed."

Another neighbor who knew the family also questioned the self-defense theory.

"Marge weighed about 300 pounds and had problems with her legs. Billy is an athletic kid, 17 years old," he said. "He had to beat her like that in self defense?"

More sinister, though, were allegations of earlier incidents in which Shrubsall's dark and violent inner demons rose frighteningly to the surface. They were ruled inadmissible as evidence by the court, and were absent from the newspaper accounts altogether.

One Niagara Falls woman said she was attacked in January 1986, when she was 14 years old.

"I got pushed down in the snow, and this young man was straddling me," the woman recalled. "He had my hands pinned behind my back. He leaned over me and tried to kiss me and said he wanted me to (perform oral sex) on him."

When the boy went to unbutton the girl's jeans, she grabbed his nose, twisted it and began screaming as loud as she could, she said. The boy got up and fled.

Months later, she saw the boy again at a youth center and recognized him as her attacker, both because of his distinctive voice and the fact that he was wearing the same clothing. It was Billy. The woman didn't tell police, thinking no one would believe her over a top student and athlete like Shrubsall. Instead, she said, her boyfriend beat him up.

In another incident, more than a year before the horrific murder of his mother, Shrubsall attended a summer basketball camp at Niagara University. Two secretaries from the school would later testify that Shrubsall stalked them and made sexual comments to them, although no charges were ever filed in the case.

"He had this intense look. It's very difficult to describe. I thought at one point, 'He hates women,'" one of the secretaries said, seemingly near tears. "For the rest of my life, if I see him near me, I will get that feeling. It's an intense fear."

The woman said Shrubsall came up behind her and said, "I want you." She said she turned and ran from the youth's "angry" gaze, and he gave chase across the campus.

"I could almost feel his breath on the back of my neck, he was that close," the woman remembered. "While we were running, he said to me, 'Turn around, you'll change your mind.'"

The two agreed not to press charges following the incident so long as Marge Shrubsall would get psychiatric help for her obviously troubled son. Later, the women were told by the basketball coach that the distraught Mrs. Shrubsall broke down in tears, sobbing and crying as she heard what her Billy was accused of doing.

In 1988, both women were horrified when they saw Shrubsall's picture in the paper after his mother's brutal murder.

"Immediately, the feelings of fear rose in me again," said the second secretary, now a retired, 71-year-old Niagara Falls resident.

Because no criminal charges had been filed in either case, they were inadmissible before the court even after they were brought to the attention of law enforcement. The baby-faced killer was out on bail in no time. He moved in with his aunt, June Epp, but his first order of business was to throw a party for 30 of his closest friends at the murder house.

The neighbors were sickened.

"He and his friends were sitting there, drinking beer and eating pizza, 15 feet from the spot where he killed his mother," one reported. "Would you be able to do that, go back into that house after what happened there?"

But to some, Billy had become a local celebrity, an infamous anti-hero living in a world he never made. He was seen driving an Olds Cutlass equipped with a vanity license plate holder reading "THE LEGEND LIVES," and when he stopped, the neighborhood kids ran up to the car to talk to him.

"Everyone has seen it," one woman said. "What kind of a kid

would run around in a car like that?"

Still, the newspapers took pains to paint the youthful killer in the best light possible. It wasn't Billy who was doing anything wrong, it was the nosy neighbors.

NIGHTMARE ON 70TH STREET: This modest brick bunglow in LaSalle became the scene of gruesome carnage when Billy Shrubsall snapped the night before his high school graduation.

Unsurprisingly, Shrubsall's attorney, Paul Cleary, championed this view.

"They're small-minded gossips who are shooting their mouths off out of total ignorance," Cleary told the *Buffalo News*. "They don't know a damned thing about how the boy feels."

His legal problems prevented his accepting scholarship offers from a number of prestigious universities, including Princeton and Penn, but Billy enrolled at nearby Niagara University and began living the carefree life of a college freshman as his case plodded through the system.

In June 1989, Shrubsall pleaded guilty to a reduced charge of manslaughter. But Cleary failed in his effort to convince Niagara County Judge Charles Hannigan that the confessed killer should be given youthful offender status and sentenced under those more lenient guidelines.

When Hannigan gave Billy an opportunity to speak, the young killer seemed tongue-tied.

"I just want to say that I loved my mother very much, your honor, and all the ... She wasn't a witch, it was nothing. I loved her very much. She was a good mother but, for 17 years, Lord, your honor, I had ... She told me to do things," he rambled.

While Cleary refrained from asking for mercy for his client on the grounds that Billy was an orphan, it wasn't by much.

"Our system mandates that if you commit a crime, you have to pay a price," he said. "Billy's already paid a big price, he's going to have to pay a much bigger price. But in this particular instance, that price should not be the total destruction of his life.

"This is the strangest, most unique case, factually, I've ever seen in my years of practicing law," he added.

The eminent Dr. Ewing argued under oath that Billy's exemplary academic record should be taken into account.

"I've evaluated hundreds of adolescents," he said. "He's the brightest one I've seen."

But Hannigan was a no-nonsense jurist of the law-and-order school, and the pleadings of the lawyer and the psychologist didn't sway him.

"Don't we as a society have a right to expect more from him because of the intellectual advantages he's been given?" Hannigan asked.

He was equally dismissive of the abuse excuse.

"Show me a kid that hasn't been spanked, hit, walloped, and I'll show you a spoiled kid," he said.

With that, he sentenced Billy to 5-to-15 years in the state penitentiary.

The appeal process began immediately, with Cleary continuing to argue that Hannigan erred in failing to grant youthful offender status to the killer.

And in November 1990, the appeals court judges agreed with him, by a 4-1 vote.

"Defendant had an excellent reputation in the community, having been first in his high school class academically, as well as editor of the yearbook and a member of the chorus, drama club, math league and student government," the judges wrote. "Prospects for the defendant's rehabilitation are good."

Billy ended up serving just 16 months for his mother's unspeakable murder. Moreover, because of the youthful offender status, his criminal record was ordered sealed from public view.

Det. Frank Coney remains outraged.

"I believe the system let the public down," Coney said. "He was quickly put back on the street after a hideous, violent murder, and more women had to suffer because of it."

Shrubsall entered an Ivy League school, the University of Pennsylvania, in 1992. He completed his courses there in 1994, one exam short of a degree, and moved out into the working world. He came back to Niagara

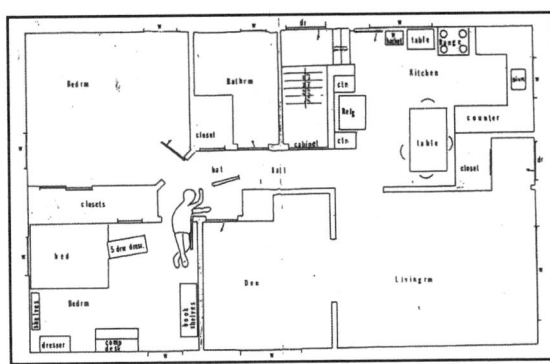

SCENE OF THE CRIME: Niagara Falls police diagram showing location of body and murder weapon in the Shrubsall residence.

Falls, where he worked briefly at a used-car lot and a restaurant.

A job as a junior stock analyst at a prominent Wall Street firm led to a move to New York City in 1995 but, like a moth to the flame, Billy would be drawn back to Niagara Falls and more trouble still.

On January 5, 1995, an attractive young woman was traveling on the New York State Thruway near Rochester when she was motioned to pull over by a man driving alongside her in a late-model Chrysler with dealer stickers and no license plates. When she stopped, the man told her he was an undercover police officer.

She said the man told her she had been speeding but she could "settle this ticket now" by going back to his car and performing oral sex on him. She stepped on the gas and fled the scene. She reported the incident to police, who then tracked the Chrysler to a Niagara Falls auto dealership where Shrubsall worked as a salesman.

Shrubsall admitted pulling the woman over but said it was to tell her something was dangling from the back of her car. New York State Trooper Anthony Domagala didn't believe the story and arrested him on a charge of felony criminal impersonation of a police officer.

"He was very educated, very smart and very smooth," the now-retired state trooper recalled.

The case fell apart when the victim refused to testify against Shrubsall after learning he'd killed his mother, Domagala said.

"She told me she didn't want to proceed with it any further, that she was scared," he said. "She was living alone as a student and felt intimidated he might know where she lived."

In August 1995, Billy was arrested again, this time on charges he had sexually abused and sodomized an underage girl who had fallen asleep at a house party. An eyewitness in the case said Billy forced the girl to perform fellatio on him.

Cops caught a break this time, as both the witness and the victim agreed to testify.

After his arraignment, Shrubsall was quickly released on bail. But it wasn't too long before he was arrested once more on a sex charge.

The victim in that case, now a Niagara Falls single mother, told police she was out for her evening walk, listening to some music on headphones, when Shrubsall approached her from the opposite direction. He said hello as they passed, but she picked up her pace when she sensed he'd turned to follow her. Suddenly, she said, he grabbed her from behind, with one arm around her waist and a hand on her buttocks.

"I was pushed over onto a grassy area off the sidewalk. He lifted me off the ground, literally," she said. "There was force. There was a lot of aggression."

The woman broke free and swung at her attacker, then chased him into a bakery parking lot, where she picked up a large stick and began yelling at him.

He ran from the scene, and a passerby told her minutes later she'd been chasing Billy Shrubsall.

"My heart just about dropped because he had been known for murdering his mother in that area, everyone knew the name," she testified. "I thought that I was crazy to have chased him."

The incident so unnerved her that, in an ironic twist, she still keeps her own baseball bat by her bed for protection, she said.

"I went into the shed when I got home after the attack, and the first thing I saw was a baseball bat," she said. "I put that baseball bat in my bedroom, and it's still there to this day."

Shrubsall later pleaded guilty to a reduced-count misdemeanor assault in the case and was sentenced to serve 90 days in the

Niagara County Jail. He was released just in time to face the far more serious felony charges of sexual abuse and sodomy stemming from his brutal house-party attack more than a year earlier.

Ironically, Judge Charles Hannigan, who oversaw Shrubsall's trial in the murder of his mother, was again presiding. And the good judge made it clear from the outset he was going to do everything in his power to ensure the ruthless predator didn't slip through the cracks in the system again.

Although many women have had cause to fear Billy Shrubsall, the two young Niagara Falls women involved in this case lived for years in a state of constant dread. It was their damning and unshakable testimony that ultimately convicted him of the most serious charges he'd faced since murdering his mother.

The 30-year-old woman he brutalized and degraded when she was just 17 said Shrubsall still haunts her nightmares. Even now, it's difficult for her to talk about the attack without shedding tears.

"I wake up in the middle of the night screaming," the woman said.

The long nightmare began on Aug. 5, 1995, when the two girls attended a house party in the Town of Niagara. The victim fell ill and went to an upstairs bedroom to lie down, only to awake in an alcoholic haze a few minutes later to find Shrubsall straddling her, touching her vagina and finally ejaculating onto her shirt.

At the time, the young girl knew nothing about Shrubsall's conviction, seven years earlier, for the gruesome murder of his mother, she said. He'd once told her his mother had beaten him repeatedly with a hot iron over his grades, and she said she had felt sorry for him.

The other young woman testified that, when she went upstairs to check on her friend 10 or 20 minutes later, it seemed as though someone was holding the bedroom door shut.

After a few seconds, Shrubsall came out of the bedroom holding up the top of his trousers. Her friend was sitting on the bed crying, she said.

"It seemed like sex was always on his mind," the witness testified. "I had a feeling that he had something he hated about women."

State police Det. Frank Panza, now retired, was assigned to investigate the case. He said his eerie feeling about Shrubsall was so strong after meeting him for the first time, he requested backup from Niagara Falls city police when he returned to Shrubsall's home the next night.

"When I left the home the first time ... I just felt personally that I was in danger," Panza testified.

Asked to sum up his opinion of Shrubsall, Panza answered with a single word.

"Evil," he said.

Things weren't looking good for the defendant, and the thought of serious prison time weighed heavy on his mind. Lawyers for both sides delivered their final arguments, and Hannigan was planning to have the jurors begin their deliberations the next day when, on May 15, Shrubsall dropped his well-planned bombshell.

That night, June Epp, Billy's aunt — who had mortgaged her home to pay her nephew's $20,000 bail — found a neat, handwritten four-page suicide note on the night stand in his room.

"Let's face it, losing means the next 8 1/3 to 25 years are spoken for," he wrote. "Years filled with rapes at the hands of HIV-infested inmates and frequent stabbings and (probable) death as an accused sex offender.

"It's all my fault. I lost for two reasons. 1) Because I allowed myself to set foot in this awful county again after graduation, and 2) because I agreed not to testify. I was a liar and a deceiver and a 'sexual predator' because I could not prove otherwise, having stood mute.

"I have nothing: no family (except for you), no friends, no girlfriend or wife, no money, no job, no prospects, meaningless education ... and mountains of debt. Most of all, no hope. I meant to do this earlier, but I haven't had the guts. Tonight I took the $5 you gave me, bought some alcohol, got drunk and walked to the Falls. To my knowledge no one has ever survived the American Falls. I don't think I will either."

It was all too perfect. Billy had said goodbye cruel world to the sad sound of violins.

But there was just one problem: Nobody believed him.

Judge Hannigan went ahead and allowed the jury to begin deliberations despite Shrubsall's absence, and a guilty verdict was promptly returned. A fugitive arrest warrant was issued, and people kept their doors and windows locked, certain in the knowledge that the depraved maniac was alive and walking the streets a free man.

"I knew he didn't do it," one neighbor said. "He loved himself too much."

Det. Coney was equally convinced the killer was alive.

"We heard many times that one person or another saw him in bars here in Niagara Falls, or in other places, but we were never able to catch him," Coney said.

Less than a month after his phony suicide, Billy Shrubsall turned up using an assumed name in Halifax, Nova Scotia, a Canadian city of a quarter-million people on the Atlantic Ocean.

Introducing himself as Ian Thor Greene, Shrubsall took up residence in a fraternity house and passed himself off as a 19-year-old college student despite his advancing age and receding hairline.

His father had been killed in a car accident near Moose Jaw, Saskatchewan, driving to see young Ian play in a youth hockey tournament, he said, while his mother died in a house fire resulting from her habit of smoking in bed. The IRA had killed his only brother in Belfast, he added.

His fraternity brothers in Halifax knew him as a bright, charming guy who made friends easily and pursued women relentlessly.

"He's the best con man I've ever met in my life. Or that I've seen on TV or heard about," said Troy Blair, who lived in the fraternity house with Billy.

"He was sexually aggressive," added another member of the fraternity, Jason MacDonald. "He had a lot of girls over."

Shrubsall's charade continued for two years. Then, early in the morning of June 22, 1998, fraternity member Mike McKeigan heard what sounded like a fight going on in Ian Greene's room downstairs. In the dimly lit hallway outside that room, McKeigan saw the man he knew as Greene sitting on top of a struggling, screaming young woman dressed only in panties.

"Help me, help me," the desperate woman cried. "He's trying to kill me!"

Frozen and speechless, McKeigan watched as his fraternity brother savagely pounded the victim with his fists, grabbed her by the ankles and dragged her into his room.

"He was choking her with both hands," McKeigan said. "It was like something out of the movies."

Greene emerged from the room, shut the door and locked it.

"Everything's under control," he said with a smile.

Halifax police called to the scene quickly linked the suspect to a series of 14 sexual assaults that had occurred in their city over the past two years. All of the Nova Scotia attacks were against women, one of whom was beaten so severely with a baseball bat she was comatose for several weeks and remains disfigured, with metal plates replacing much of what was once her skull. In another case, he was identified as the man who robbed a teenage girl and forced her to perform oral sex on him.

But police soon realized that no such person as Ian Thor Greene really existed. Or ever had. They pressed the suspect for his true identity, but he remained uncooperative.

Coney was working the graveyard shift on the night of July 24, 1998, when he got a call from a Niagara Falls man who had just watched a Canadian news program on television. There had been a story about a violent sexual predator who had been captured in Nova Scotia. The video captured a clear image of the suspect's face.

"It was Billy Shrubsall, Frank," the caller said.

Coney immediately had a set of Shrubsall's fingerprints and mugshots sent to the Halifax police, and Billy's identity was quickly confirmed.

The case took nearly two years to come to trial, but the forensic evidence and eyewitness testimony against the defendant were overwhelming. After Shrubsall was found guilty in three of the sadistic attacks, prosecutors asked the court to declare him a "dangerous repeat offender." Under Canadian law, such a designation allows the court to impose an indeterminate sentence, one that could mean life in prison without parole.

Although Shrubsall's convictions in Canada carried a combined 30 years of prison time, and he still faced sentencing in Niagara Falls for his 1996 in-absentia conviction on felony sexual assault and sodomy charges, lawmen on both sides of the border were eager to ensure Shrubsall never again posed a threat to society.

To achieve this end, evidence of past misdeeds — everything from the savage 1988 baseball-bat slaying of his mother to allegations he once cheated in a high school track meet — was painstakingly collected and presented to the court.

A parade of more than 50 prosecution witnesses, many from Niagara Falls, made the trip to Nova Scotia to testify. And the portrait of Shrubsall that emerged was one of a psychopathic, cold-blooded monster.

Shrubsall, who ballooned to 250 pounds in the months following his arrest, passed his days in the Halifax courtroom of Nova Scotia Justice Felix Cacchione wearing a too-tight blue suit, doodling on a legal pad and paying scant attention to the testimony presented against him. His nights were spent in forced isolation, having been spit on and threatened as a sex offender by other inmates.

As witness after witness offered tearful testimony of their brutal encounters with the sadistic defendant, and law enforcement officers from a half-dozen police agencies painstakingly presented the often shocking details in each of the cases, Shrubsall seemed to become even more detached. At one point, he went so far as to instruct his Canadian attorney, Lonny Queripel, to inform the judge he wouldn't appeal the verdict, an apparent attempt to gain the court's sympathy.

Queripel did what he could during cross examination and fought to keep all evidence of his client's U.S. activities out of the dangerous-offender hearing, particularly in cases where Shrubsall wasn't convicted.

But Queripel had little success, leading him to question the motives of the women and cops who testified. In the 1995 police-impersonation case, for example, the lawyer argued that the whole thing boiled down to the woman's word against his client's.

"You don't have any further evidence to offer to this court today bolstering her version or weakening Mr. Shrubsall's?" Queripel asked the arresting officer, Anthony Domagala, on cross examination.

"That's correct," the state trooper replied.

Any small headway Queripel might have made along these lines was all but erased by the testimony of a platoon of court-appointed psychiatrists who described Shrubsall as a psychotic personality and declared it highly unlikely he would ever stop committing violent crimes against women.

"If there was ever an individual who fits the 'dangerous offender' category, it's Billy Shrubsall," one of the experts later told a reporter. "This time, it's finally caught up to him."

In January 2002, after more than six months of testimony, Justice Cacchione handed down the indeterminate sentence sought by the prosecution as appropriate for such a violent and sadistic offender. Although he was able to escape and successfully evade law enforcement for two years following his 1996 Niagara Falls conviction, and served just 16 months for his mother's gruesome slaying, it is unlikely Shrubsall will ever again see the light of day as a free man.

The sentencing made headlines across North America, but nowhere did the case serve to dredge up frightening and often bitter memories more than in Niagara Falls, the scene of Shrubsall's early depredations.

"Hopefully, he'll be in jail for a long time up there and, if he ever gets out, we'll put him back in jail for a long time here," Niagara County District Attorney Matthew Murphy said. "It's just unfortunate to think how much of this might have been avoided had Judge Hannigan's original sentence been allowed to stand."

Dr. Charles P. Ewing, the forensic psychologist who helped free Shrubsall by predicting he would pose no threat to society after his mother's murder, now routinely declines comment on the case. He is available, however, to testify as an "expert witness" on behalf of other children accused of killing one or both parents, or for the desperate housewife who claims murdering her hubby as he slept was the only way out of an abusive relationship.

All for a fee, of course.

Shrubsall's attorney in the original murder case, Paul Cleary, still defends the system that set the convicted killer free to begin in earnest his career as a depraved, woman-hating rapist.

"It wasn't the system's fault, it was Billy Shrubsall who failed the system," Cleary told a reporter. "Four judges who never met this kid stuck their necks out for him, showed some compassion, gave him a chance to start a whole new life.

"He was a brilliant kid. He had great opportunities. He had an Ivy League education. He should be on Wall Street somewhere, making millions of dollars. He threw all that away.

"Don't blame the system. It's the most disappointing thing I've seen in all my years as a lawyer," Cleary added.

Det. Frank Coney takes a harsher view. Even today, the veteran cop who relentlessly pursued Shrubsall for more than a dozen years can't or won't disguise the hint of bitterness in his voice when discussing the case.

"This is a truly diabolical individual," he said. "He's been laughing at the system all along, starting with the day he killed his mother. But now he's in jail up there in Canada, I don't think he's laughing anymore."

THEY CALLED HIM
THE UNDERTAKER

By Mike Hudson

Today it stands, empty and forgotten, at the rundown corner of Niagara Street and Portage Road in what used to be a fashionable section of town. To those who remember, it serves as a monument to a powerful regime long since passed. A reminder of better times for a city seen by many as having fallen so far, so fast, into the abyss.

In 1997, it was bought for back taxes by a local entrepreneur who speculated its proximity to a proposed mega-mall would make it worth more than the $15,000 he paid.

The Magaddino Memorial Chapel. If only the walls could talk. The FBI found $30,000 stashed there when they raided the place in 1969, one of a series of raids designed to break the back of organized crime in Western New York.

To break the back of Stefano Magaddino, that is, proprietor of the funeral home and one of the most powerful crime lords in U.S. history.

"When I was a kid, they used to say there was more than one body in some of them caskets that came out of there," Falls resident Margie Blazing said.

First publicly identified as head of the Buffalo Mafia in a May 1952 "Look" magazine article, Magaddino figured prominently in the televised Senate Rackets Committee hearings that featured the testimony of mobster-turned-government stool pigeon Joe Valachi.

When told Magaddino had been referred to as a "bag of wind" by another witness, Valachi laughed.

"He's no bag of wind, senator," he said. "He is boss since the late '20s. If he was a bag of wind, he would have been out of there a long time ago."

Magaddino was also named in the 1966 New York State Commission on Investigation report.

"Magaddino is in absolute control of all illegal operations pertaining to organized crime in Western New York and Southern Ontario," the report stated.

To many who knew him in Niagara Falls, however, "Steve," or "the Old Man," was a benevolent figure who would buy a round for the house or leave the waitress who served him dinner a tip larger than the check. A

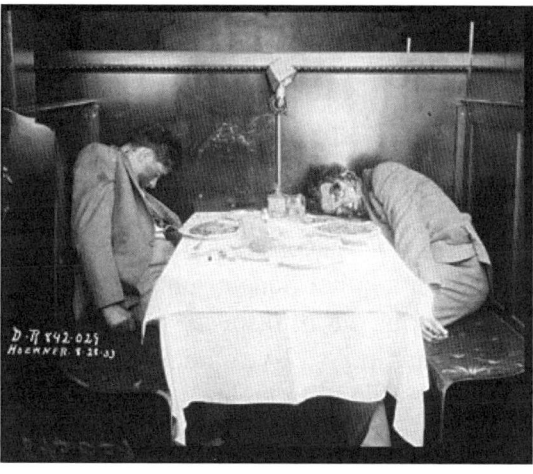

MOB JUSTICE? While many in Niagara Falls saw him as a benevolent, almost avuncular character, federal law enforcement officials said Stefano Magaddino was a cold-blooded killer who left a trail of mangled bodies wherever he went.

heavyset, bull-necked man with a round face, he was a neat, conservative dresser who shunned flashy clothes and other traditional gangster trappings.

"In one way or another, he touched everyone's life," said Flo Acotto, who owned the Press Box restaurant on Niagara Street. "They never bothered the mediocre people, only the ones who were bothering them."

Acotto was a childhood friend of Magaddino's daughter.

"They were nice people, the whole family," she said. "I went to school with Steve's daughter, Connie. If you told her one day that was a pretty dress she was wearing, you know what would happen? The next day, she'd come to school with the dress in a bag and give it to you. I saw her do it."

Terry Kilpatrick, who grew up in the Falls when Magaddino was a powerful force, agreed.

"It was good when the Old Man was running things," he said. "They took care of things and they didn't go out looking for trouble."

But to federal law enforcement officials, Magaddino was a ruthless killer whose criminal empire stretched from Toronto to Cleveland. The 1966 Crime Commission report stated the criminal enterprise centered on gambling, loan sharking, drug smuggling and extortion. Such was the Old Man's power that in 1988, nearly 15 years after his death, mob turncoat Angelo Leonardo referred to the Buffalo La Cosa Nostra as "the Magaddino Family" in testimony before yet another Senate subcommittee.

That was out of respect.

Magaddino's 52-year tenure as head of a Mafia family is a record less likely to be broken than Joe DiMaggio's 56-game consecutive hitting streak in professional baseball. Allan May, a Cleveland-based investigative journalist specializing in organized crime, has called Magaddino "the grand old man of the Cosa Nostra."

And in his front-page 1974 obituary in the *Niagara Falls Gazette*, Magaddino was described as "the man who ran everything in Niagara Falls but the Cascades."

Don Stefano Magaddino was born Oct. 10, 1891, in Castellammare del Golfo, a picturesque Sicilian village near Palermo noted primarily in this country for the disproportionate number of organized crime figures it produced. Along with his brothers, Pietro and Antonio, Magaddino became involved in the clannish, underground world of the Sicilian Mafia. A feud between the Magaddinos and another set of brothers, the Buccellatos, resulted in Pietro's murder in 1920. Stefano and Antonio fled Sicily for New York City, but the trouble continued.

On Aug. 16, 1921, Stefano Magaddino was arrested in connection with the shooting death of a Buccellato man in Avon, N.J. The warrant claimed Magaddino "acted in concert with other persons" in the killing, but the charge was later dropped for lack of evidence.

It was the last time Magaddino would spend a night behind bars and, for nearly a half-century, the last time law enforcement would bother him at all.

Later that summer, Magaddino and an associate, Gaspar Milazzo, were nearly gunned down in an ambush as they exited a

Brooklyn store. The two men decided to leave New York, Milazzo for Detroit and Magaddino for Buffalo.

Each man would become the head of organized crime in their adopted hometowns, although Milazzo's reign in Detroit was cut short by that city's notorious Purple Gang. He died in a hail of bullets in 1930.

Newspaper obituaries state Magaddino worked briefly for a produce company in Buffalo after his arrival, but he soon moved to Niagara Falls. It was the height of Prohibition, and opportunities to

BOSS OF BOSSES: Stefano Magaddino maintained a stranglehold on Niagara Falls for nearly a half-century. His influence in the underworld spread to Montreal, New York City and beyond.

make money were unlimited for a young immigrant willing to smuggle booze across the border from Canada. The profits were enormous, and he used them to establish a number of legitimate businesses, including a linen-supply company and the funeral home.

His involvement in the latter enterprise earned him the underworld moniker "The Undertaker."

Back in New York, a war broke out between the city's two most powerful Mafia chieftains, Salvatore Maranzano and Joe "The Boss" Masseria. Fought over territory and power, the conflict became known as the "Castellammarese War," after the hometown of Maranzano, Magaddino and others involved in it.

Magaddino and other young mobsters like Charles "Lucky"

Luciano saw the war as an opportunity. Although he reportedly backed the efforts of his cousin, Joe Bonanno, on behalf of Masseria, it is unlikely Magaddino shed any tears on April 15, 1931, when Masseria was whacked while enjoying dinner at a Coney Island spaghetti house.

Six months later, Maranzano was shot and stabbed to death in his Park Avenue office by assassins dressed in police uniforms and dispatched by Luciano's friend, Benjamin "Bugsy" Siegel.

With the old bosses out of the way, the stage was set for Magaddino and others of his generation to take control. Tired of the bad publicity and police attention generated by the Castellammarese War, the country's most powerful and influential gangsters — including Magaddino, his cousin Joe Bonanno of New York, Vito Genovese, Joe Profaci, Thomas Lucchese and Carlo Gambino, also of New York, and Frank Nitti of Chicago — established the Commission, the ruling body of La Cosa Nostra in the United States.

Its existence was a closely guarded secret until Joe Valachi began testifying before Senate subcommittees and talking to writers in the late 1950s and early 1960s.

According to Valachi, the purpose of the organization was to prevent feuds by establishing territories for the various crime families, which at the height of their power numbered 26 across the country. No "made," or initiated, member of the Cosa Nostra was allowed to kill another without permission, and disputes were to be settled in the boardroom rather than on the street. The Commission met formally once every five years to re-elect the heads of the families.

Magaddino's second-in-command was John Montana of Buffalo. In addition to owning the largest fleet of taxicabs in Western New York, Montana was twice elected to the Buffalo Common Council and once named "Man of the Year" by the National Junior Chamber of Commerce.

The men were partners in the Empire State Brewery in Olean, N.Y., and their relationship was further strengthened when Magaddino's son, Peter, married Montana's daughter, Frances.

There were some problems, but they were dealt with. According to Ray Porello, author of "The Rise and Fall of the Cleveland Mafia," an Ohio gang came to Niagara Falls shortly before the end of Prohibition in an attempt to muscle in on Magaddino's bootlegging business. One of them went home in a box; the rest left voluntarily.

YOU PLUG 'EM, WE PLANT 'EM: The Magaddino Memorial Chapel stands deserted at the corner of Niagara Street and Portage Road. It was rumored that some caskets leaving the funeral home held more than one body.

Occasionally, a gambler or loan sharking customer would fall behind in his payments, only to wind up sitting across from the Don at a table in the back of a Pierce Avenue social club he used as an office.

"I don't have the money," they'd say. "You can't get blood out of a stone."

"No," he'd tell them. "But a stone can be broken."

On May 19, 1936, a bomb intended for Magaddino exploded next door, at the home of his sister and brother-in-law. The sister, Arcangela Longo, was killed and her three young daughters injured in the blast.

"My mother dragged me over to see it," Flo Acotto said. "Everybody in town went to see."

Newspaper accounts at the time speculated about an ongoing feud between rival gambling factions in Buffalo and Niagara Falls.

"Falls police are not reticent in admitting they are looking for reprisals, but said today they are in the dark as to where the reprisals would break out or in what element," a front-page article reported.

They didn't have to wait long. Later that summer, when a Buffalo hood named Frank Lotempio was found shot to death, Magaddino was questioned but never charged.

By the end of the 1930s, and in the decades that followed, Magaddino was firmly in control, and Niagara Falls enjoyed a peace and prosperity it had never known. Workers earned good money at Hooker Chemical, Carborundum and Bell Aviation and, to most people, a little gambling seemed like a harmless bit of recreation.

"People like to gamble, so what?" Terry Kilpatrick said. "They didn't bother a soul."

The Magaddino family, including Stefano, his brother, Antonio, son Peter and cousin Peter, were respected as successful business-men in the community.

Acotto, who opened her restaurant in 1958, remembers the family well.

"Pete the Bull, he was Steve's cousin, he used to come in here when we first opened. Back then, you had to show you sold so much food before you could get your liquor license, and he'd have lunch and throw down ten, twenty dollars and say, 'Ring it up, get your license.'"

When the license was awarded, the beer, linen and amusement concessions were assigned to the different family businesses and delivered on Magaddino trucks. Acotto knew that no one would be so foolish as to walk out on a lunch tab without paying.

But for Stefano Magaddino, the bucolic times were about to come to an end.

According to Valachi, it was Magaddino's idea to hold the 1957 Commission meeting at a cabin owned by Pennsylvania Mafia chieftain Joseph Barbara in Apalachin, N.Y. Usually, they met in Chicago or New York City.

Local state troopers, suspicious of the fancy cars and out-of-state license plates, raided the place.

A total of 58 mobsters were arrested, including Magaddino's brother, Antonio, and close associates John Montana, Joe "The Wolf" Di Carlo and Rosario Carlisi.

Magaddino's driver's license and other personal effects were found at the scene, but he eluded the dragnet.

For law enforcement, Apalachin provided the first glimpse into the shadowy world of La Cosa Nostra. For the gangsters, it was an unmitigated disaster. And many blamed Magaddino personally.

In 1958, someone threw a hand grenade through the kitchen window of Magaddino's Lewiston home. Interestingly, the explosive had been removed from the device before it was thrown, leading some to speculate the incident was an indication of bad feelings associated with Apalachin. But this was never confirmed.

Security around the neighborhood became tight, according to former Niagara Falls city councilman Bruce Battaglia.

"My father-in-law wanted to buy a house up there, and the real estate agent asked how he was financing it," Battaglia said. "He was an old Polish guy, saved his money, and said he'd be paying cash.

"The real estate guy said he'd have to check with the Old Man to see if it was all right. Apparently it was, because they called my father-in-law a couple of days later and closed the deal."

Magaddino was questioned by authorities in connection with the murder of Albert Agueci, a two-bit drug runner killed in 1961.

Along with his brother, Vito, Albert Agueci was involved in smuggling heroin into the United States from Montreal. Born and raised in Sicily, the brothers had Magaddino's blessing and paid him a percentage of their drug profits until they were arrested on narcotics charges in New York City.

Magaddino reneged on his promise to provide support, and Albert Agueci's wife was forced to mortgage the family home for bail. Agueci started making noises about getting even and, on Nov. 23, 1961, his mutilated body was found on a farm outside Rochester. His jaw had been shattered and half his teeth knocked out. An estimated 30 pounds of flesh had been cut from his bones before the killers strangled him with a clothesline. The body was then soaked with gasoline and set on fire.

Vito Agueci became a government witness in the wake of his brother's gruesome murder, but his testimony was never enough to put the Old Man behind bars.

As often as not in those days, the Old Man could be found lunching at Little Italy's best restaurant, the Como on Pine Avenue, where he and his lieutenants had a special table back by the kitchen.

"They'd come in one by one, two by two, you know, and when they sat down they'd drop a fork or something on the floor, so they could look under the table and make sure there wasn't any microphones," said owner Mario Antonacci. "It was like a ritual they had."

In New York City, it was the time of the "Banana War," involving Magaddino's cousin Joe Bonanno. Related by blood, the two had grown distant, and Bonanno's interests in Montreal were getting dangerously close to Toronto, Magaddino's territory.

On Oct. 21, 1964, Bonanno was walking down Park Avenue in Manhattan when he was abducted by two men who forced him into a car. Federal authorities investigating the case questioned Magaddino's brother, Antonio, and son, Peter, in connection with the kidnapping, but no charges were filed.

Bonanno was released unharmed a short while later and "retired" to Arizona, where he lived until his death from natural causes in 2002.

The afternoon of Nov. 26, 1968, was cold and rainy in Niagara Falls, in all respects a typical late-autumn day on which the extraordinary was about to happen.

People passing by the corner of 28th Street and Ferry Avenue were startled to see a Niagara Falls Police Department cruiser, accompanied by a pair of black sedans, pull over a slow-moving white Cadillac and arrest its 77-year-old driver.

The surprise turned to shock when they realized the driver was no ordinary senior citizen on his way to the grocery store.

It was Stefano Magaddino, a figure who had come to be respected and feared by law enforcement and the underworld alike as perhaps the most powerful organized crime boss in the country.

Federal, state and local authorities simultaneously raided Magaddino's home, his son Peter's home and the funeral parlor, ultimately arresting nine men on federal charges of conspiracy and violation of the Interstate Transportation in Aid of Racketeering Act.

In addition to Stefano and Peter Magaddino, Benjamin Nicoletti

Sr., Sam Pugalese, Gino Monaco, Pasquale "Patsy" Passaro, Augustine Rizzo, Louis Tavano, Michael Farella and Benjamin "Sonny" Nicoletti Jr. were picked up. All except the Old Man were taken to Buffalo, where they were locked up in lieu of bail ranging from $7,500 to $100,000. Because of his health, Stefano Magaddino was confined to house arrest at his home, under 24-hour watch by a team of four marshals. Newspaper reporters quickly dubbed the jailed men the "Niagara Falls Nine" and covered the story eagerly.

In a suitcase under Peter Magaddino's bed, police found more than $500,000. Another $30,000 was stashed at the funeral home.

Peter's wife, Frances, was quoted in a "Time" magazine article about the raids.

"He said we didn't even have enough money to go to Florida," she said.

A sawed-off shotgun, an automatic pistol, a revolver and bags of wrapped coins were also seized.

FBI Agent Neil Welch told reporters that Peter Magaddino and Benjamin Nicoletti Sr. were arrested shortly after completing a meeting at the Round the Clock restaurant on Main Street. The pair met every Tuesday night at different locations around the city to discuss the week's gambling take, Welch said.

But the euphoria initially felt by the lawmen was short-lived. Federal charges against Magaddino and the Niagara Nine were later dropped by U.S. District Court Judge John O. Henderson, because law enforcement agencies refused to name an informant and the wiretaps used in gathering evidence had been illegal.

The entire episode served to mark the beginning of the end for the Old Man, however. Although it would be another six years before Magaddino would finally succumb to heart disease, those who knew him could detect a change.

Danny Cipolitti, owner of La Bruschetta restaurant on Niagara Falls Boulevard, remembers the era well.

"His mind was going by then and, during the week, Don Stefano would come walking down Pine Avenue going into all the businesses, the dry cleaner, the barber, the butcher shop, and he'd have a black bag with him. He'd go up to the counter and open the bag, and the people, whatever they had in the till, would just put it in the bag," he said. "On Saturday morning, the son, Peter, would come and go into all the places and ask, 'How much did the Old Man take you for?' and he'd pull out a wad of bills and pay the people back."

Today, Cipolitti laughs at the memory. In Niagara Falls, his is a sweet story.

Local attorney Patrick Berrigan crossed paths with Magaddino in the early '70s, while working for the Runals law firm. One of the firm's clients was "Life" magazine.

"They had been sued for libel in California for a story they'd done linking the mayor of San Francisco to the Mob and they asked us to get a deposition from Stefano," he said. "The last thing he wanted to do was to give us a deposition about the inner workings of the Mafia, and he kept checking in and out of the hospital to avoid us. We had private detectives following him and we found he went bowling every night at 3 a.m., but before we could get to him, the case was resolved."

Stefano Magaddino died of a heart attack on July 19, 1974, at the age of 82 in St. Mary's Hospital in Lewiston. His death was front-page news in Western New York and made headlines around the country.

"When Don Stefano died, I went to his funeral," Terry Kilpatrick said. "People said, 'There's going to be FBI there,' but I didn't care. He was a good man and I paid my respects."

Following the Old Man's death, federal law enforcement officials say various factions fought for control of the empire he'd built. In southern Ontario, Johnny "Pops" Papalia reportedly ran the Canadian end of the operation until his murder in 1997.

On this side of the river, a power struggle had begun even before his death. John Cammilleri, described by government informant Ron Fino as a corrupt official of Laborers Local 210 in Buffalo, died in a hail of bullets in May 1974, while crossing the street outside the Roseland restaurant in Buffalo after attending the wake of another hood, Frankie "Blaze" LoTempio.

The FBI later reported the Don's death sparked a wave of 15 mob-related murders that lasted into the mid-1980s. According to

Fino's testimony before a Senate subcommittee investigating the ties between the Mafia and the Laborers International Union of North America, former Magaddino lieutenant Joseph "Lead Pipe Joe" Todaro took control of the Buffalo family in 1984.

The days when Stefano Magaddino was "boss of bosses" in Western New York were over, but the man himself was to become the target of yet another federal investigation. And this wasn't for anything as mundane as bookmaking or simple murder.

In 1979, the House Assassinations Committee convened to take a new look at the deaths of John F. Kennedy, Robert Kennedy and Martin Luther King Jr. FBI wiretap information revealed Magaddino to be one of the Cosa Nostra leaders who talked about the need to kill JFK prior to the assassination.

In a conversation recorded in October 1963, Magaddino became agitated when another mobster remarked that President Kennedy "should drop dead."

"They should kill the whole family, the mother and father, too," Magaddino shouted. "When he talks, he talks like a mad dog!"

"The comment was followed by a string of obscenities by Stefano Magaddino," the FBI report states.

In a second wiretap, four days after the shooting in Dallas, two gangsters are heard laughing and congratulating each other about Kennedy's death. Don Stefano cautioned the men "not to joke openly about the president's murder."

"You can be sure that the police spies will be watching carefully to see what we think and say about this," he told them.

In the end, the closest the committee got to pinning the century's most infamous homicide on the Old Man was to conclude that "the (Cosa Nostra) Commission was not involved, but the committee could not preclude the involvement" of any individual members of organized crime.

Once again, the feds never laid a glove on Stefano Magaddino.

SLOWLY I TURNED ...

By Rebecca Hudson

WHY, COITANLY! These knuckleheads performed the 'Niagara Falls' routine in 1944's 'Gents Without Cents.'

Tell a non-resident you're from Niagara Falls, and the likely response will be, "Niagara Falls! Slowly I turned ... step by step ... inch by inch ..."

Where'd that come from? Some remember it as an old Abbott and Costello or Three Stooges routine. Others may recall it from an episode of "I Love Lucy."

They're all right.

The skit, which was well known on the vaudeville circuit, goes something like this: A bedraggled man buttonholes a stranger and tells him a tale of betrayal and vengeance. A rogue seduced his sweetheart. He trailed the miscreant from town to town, finally catching up with him in Niagara Falls, where he pummeled him mercilessly. The hearer of the story haplessly says the magic words, "Niagara Falls," causing the man to turn on him and mete out the same punishment.

Sometimes a different town was the red-flag word. Abbott and Costello performed the "Pokomoko" version in their 1944 film, "Lost in a Harem." The improbable storyline revolves around the pair traveling to Arabia to recover the Jimmy Dorsey Orchestra, which has been hypnotized into playing only for the villain. They pose as Hollywood talent scouts. At one point, they end up locked in a jail cell with a lunatic, who does the "Slowly I Turned" routine.

That same year, the Three Stooges incorporated it into their short feature, "Gents Without Cents." In this episode, the Stooges are out-of-work actors who meet three dancing girls in similar circumstances. They all get a job in a show, where they perform the routine. The Stooges marry the ladies and honeymoon in (where else?) Niagara Falls. This time, Curly is the Stooge who exclaims "Niagara Falls!" making himself the target of Moe and Larry's wrath.

JOEY FAYE: From second banana to Fruit of the Loom grape. Comic and veteran vaudevillian Faye claimed authorship of 'Slowly I Turned' in its many formats.

The venerable routine reappeared in an episode of "I Love Lucy" aired in 1952. Ricky needs both a ballerina and a comic to be in his floorshow at the Tropicana. Lucy, as usual, is clamoring to participate. Ricky sends her to a ballet teacher. Lucy klutzes it up, hurts her leg and hires someone to teach her a vaudeville routine instead. A typical misunderstanding occurs when Ethel tells Lucy that the show needs an emergency substitute performer. Lucy goes and performs a vaudeville routine in the ballet, walloping the dancers and causing general lunacy and mayhem.

This little skit, and its centerpiece phrase, have become so well known that its authorship would seem to be lost in the mists of time, like an old folk ballad.

Extensive research (i.e., Web-surfing) has revealed that comic Joey Faye claimed authorship of "Slowly I Turned" in its many formats. Born Joseph Palladino in 1909 on Manhattan's Lower East Side, he appeared in burlesque and vaudeville shows, usually as a sidekick to the star, often Phil Silvers. He was in 36 Broadway shows, including "Man of La Mancha" as Sancho Panza, and dozens of movies. He had his own series, "The Joey Faye Frolics," in 1950, and appeared as well in other television shows, such as "The Real McCoys," "Perry Mason" and "Maude." His most recent claim to fame was as the green grape in the Fruit of the Loom underwear commercials. He continued to work until well into his 80s and died in 1997.

Finally, the mystery has been solved. But people will continue to use the phrase at appropriate moments and enjoy its several film performances without knowing or caring about its source. It has become an acknowledged part of American popular culture, and that is a greater accomplishment than having your name appended to a bit of comic business.

DEATH AT
HORSESHOE FALLS
By Richard Hudson

Big Ed Delahanty was one of the greatest sluggers baseball would ever see. But when his body washed up below the Horseshoe Falls on July 9, 1903, a new kind of legend was born, a legend that would forever overshadow his achievements. Yet for almost 100 years, the true story of Delahanty's unusual death has never been reported accurately.

In the summer of 1903, Delahanty was the defending American League batting champion, hitting a solid .333 for Washington. He was in his 16th season as a professional baseball player, one of five brothers to make it to the majors. Delahanty was just 35 years old.

But after missing a game in Cleveland, his hometown, Delahanty was suspended from the team. Delahanty drank as hard as he hit, and on July 2, he boarded a train in Detroit, apparently heading for New York to rejoin his teammates.

He continued to drink along the way. That night, he became hostile. Brandishing a straight razor, threatening some passengers, Delahanty violently pulled a woman from her berth by her ankles. He had gone too far, and the passengers took action.

Several of the passengers went looking for someone in charge and eventually found conductor John Cole. They told Cole they needed protection from this drunken, crazy man, and the conductor went to investigate.

Cole took with him several trainmen in hopes of quelling the situation. But when they arrived on the scene, Delahanty was too far gone to reason with. Cole ordered the train to be stopped and pushed Delahanty down the long hallway leading to the rear exit. The train now was at Bridgeburg, on the Canadian side of the Niagara River across from Buffalo.

Cole shoved Delahanty off the train, handed him his hat and pointed in the direction of the station.

"And don't make any trouble, you know you're still in Canada," the conductor warned.

"I don't care whether I'm in Canada or dead," responded Delahanty.

Then the train, Michigan Central No. 6, disappeared into the night. Delahanty was left standing on the International Bridge, drunk and with thoughts of death on his mind. The river roared by just 20 feet below him.

It was almost 11 p.m., and Sam Kingston was on duty as bridge guard, a job that paid $1.74 a day. He had just left the telegraph office on the Canadian side when he spotted a man on the bridge, he later claimed.

Oddly, Kingston paid no attention to the stranger and continued his rounds. The guard simply watched as another train passed over the bridge, which extended to Squaw Island and across Black Rock Harbor.

A few minutes later, Kingston walked toward the center of the single-track railroad drawbridge. He was shocked when he spotted the man standing to the side of the tracks, as there was no foot walk on the bridge.

Kingston recognized the stranger as the same man he had seen just 10 minutes or so earlier. This time, he decided to approach the man, who was leaning against a pillar, staring into the raging waters below.

Kingston called out to the stranger, flashing his bullseye lantern in the man's face. He was unaware he was shining a light on one of baseball's greats. As far as Kingston was concerned, this was just another man in a blue suit.

"Take that lantern away or I'll break your face," Delahanty snarled, peering into the light.

After Delahanty spoke, Kingston realized the man was drunk. He knew he had to do something, and made an awkward attempt to grab Delahanty. This attempt permanently sealed the baseball legend's fate. It's uncertain whether Big Ed fell or jumped, but within seconds of the guard trying to grab him, Delahanty was in the river.

The drawbridge was open, with the freighter Ossion Bedell passing beneath on the river. But no one on the ship heard or saw anything. Kingston later said he heard the man calling out for help. But did he take action? No.

Instead, the guard turned, picked up Delahanty's derby off the tracks, put it on his own head and continued on his rounds.

DEATH BRIDGE: Like many before him and since, baseball legend Ed Delahanty found out he was no match for the mighty Niagara River. He was killed and his body washed over the falls after taking a tumble on the International Railroad Bridge near Buffalo.

He didn't report the incident until the next morning. Around the time Kingston reported what had happened, a train carrying Delahanty's team, the Washington Senators, was passing over the same bridge.

Meanwhile, Delahanty's body was making the long journey down the Niagara River. It was Fourth of July weekend, and Niagara Falls was packed. The estimated 15,000 tourists failed to notice Delahanty's corpse as it plummeted over the Horseshoe Falls.

Seven days later, Delahanty's body was found by William LeBland, a dock worker at the Maid of the Mist landing on the Ontario side of the gorge. The body was badly damaged, the left leg nearly severed after being struck by the famous sightseeing boat's propeller, and his stomach was split open, the intestines hanging out. Other than a silk necktie, shoes and socks, the dead man's clothes had been stripped off by the plummet over the falls.

After being examined by Ontario police and the coroner's office, the body was shipped back to Cleveland for burial. That's when rumors began to fly. No writer at the time wanted to say that this national hero died because he was a drunken fool. The

HALL OF FAME: The baseball world was shocked by news of Delahanty's 1903 death at Niagara Falls. His body was discovered by a dock worker at the Maid of the Mist landing.

lack of money and jewelry on the body led to whispers of foul play. The dime-novel writers weren't concerned with the fact that most bodies that go over the falls are found with barely any clothes on, let alone money or jewelry.

Delahanty's brother, Frank, fueled speculation that the bridge guard, Sam Kingston, had pushed the baseball legend from the International Bridge after robbing him. But Kingston, a man of 70, would have been unlikely to get the better of Big Ed, even in a drunken condition.

The truth is, Ed Delahanty, who had a lifetime batting average of .346, the fourth best of all time, was a wild man.

"Men who met him had to admit he was a handsome fellow, although there was an air about him that indicated he was a roughneck at heart and no man to tamper with," wrote baseball scribe Robert Smith. "He had that wide-eyed, half-smiling, ready-for-anything look that is characteristic of a certain type of Irishman. He had a towering impatience, too, and a taste for liquor and excitement. He created plenty of excitement for opponents and spectators when he laid his tremendous bat against a pitch."

Delahanty was born in Cleveland in 1867. He grew to stand 6-foot-1 and weighed in at 170 pounds. His broad shoulders were always noticed.

He started his professional baseball career playing for Mansfield in the Ohio State League in 1887. He played second base and hit an impressive .355. The next year, Delahanty moved to Wheeling and played in the Tri-State League, where his average grew to a whopping .408. As a result, he gained a lot of attention, and his contract was bought by the Philadelphia Phillies.

But Philadelphia didn't work out for Delahanty at first. His average dropped to .228, and he was a joke at second base. Big Ed worked hard, though, and over the next three years, his average rose steadily. His fielding skills also improved when the Phillies, in 1891, placed Delahanty in the outfield. He quickly became a phenomenal outfielder.

HERE LIES ED, DEAD: Delahanty's grieving brother, Frank, took the Hall of Famer's mangled body back to his hometown of Cleveland, where it was buried in Calvary Cemetery.

This is when Delahanty's star really began to shine bright. In 1892, he hit .306, leading the National League with 21 triples.

Over the next four years, Delahanty hit .368, .407, .404 and .397. And he was part of an all-star outfield, with "Sliding Billy" Hamilton stationed in center field and Sam Thompson covering right. This whole outfield would eventually find its way into the Hall of Fame.

On June 16, 1894, Delahanty went six-for-six. Then on July 13, 1896, Delahanty secured his place among the greats of baseball. In a game in Chicago, Delahanty hit four consecutive home runs. All inside the park! He was only the second man ever to do so.

The more success he had, it seemed, the more Delahanty sought to destroy himself. Booze became a constant in his life. He quickly was becoming a dependent alcoholic. Fifty years before James Dean and Marilyn Monroe, Delahanty was perfecting the art of being an out-of-control celebrity.

He continued to play well despite his love of the bottle. In 1899, Delahanty ruled the NL with a .410 batting average. Only Ty Cobb and Rogers Hornsby have since managed to achieve as high an average.

That same year, Delahanty dominated the NL with 238 hits, 55 doubles and 137 RBIs. During the next two seasons, he continued to lead the league, smashing 38 doubles in 1901. This was the fourth time he took the title for the most doubles in his league.

Delahanty was growing restless and, when the budding American League offered him almost double what the NL was paying him, he jumped. He went from $2,500 to $4,000 a year, big money at a time when athletes weren't paid much to begin with. Big Ed now was a Washington Senator. And in the summer of 1902, Delahanty batted .376, becoming the leading hitter in his new league. At the age of 35, his statistics were staggering, with 2,597 hits, 522 doubles, 185 triples, 101 home runs, 1,599 runs scored and 1,464 RBIs. But the end was near. Whether Delahanty knew this, we can never be sure. The best clues are found in the newspaper articles during the weeks following the discovery of Delahanty's body.

According to articles in the *Niagara Falls Gazette*, Delahanty was despondent during his final days. Before leaving Detroit, where he was ejected from a club for drunkenness, he wrote his wife in Washington, telling her of a life insurance policy he had bought. He also wrote that things looked so bad for him that he hoped the train would jump off the tracks and be "dashed to pieces," he along with it.

Then he got on the train.

When a psychotic Delahanty got himself kicked off a train and jumped or fell into the Niagara River, he secured his place in history. Life made Ed Delahanty a superstar. His death made him a legend.

WHO KILLED
JIMMY LIBRIZE?

By Mike Hudson

Niagara Falls was a different sort of place back in 1969. A prosperous city of 100,000 souls, with plants like Bell Aerospace, Hooker Chemical and Carborundum fueling a booming economy that now seems a distant and sometimes bitter memory.

Don Stefano Magaddino ran the Mob and much else from his funeral-home fortress at Niagara Street and Portage Road, and Mayor E. Dent Lackey had yet to begin the program of urban renewal that would leave the city's downtown a devastated hulk.

Falls Street was a bustling, if down at the heels, district of old-time shops, hotels and restaurants, while the nightclubs on Third Street enjoyed a never-ending stream of revelers.

And then there was Jimmy LiBrize, the diminutive but always flamboyant criminal defense attorney whose penchant for show-manship, both in the courtroom and as part of the city's thriving nightlife, made him something of a local character, if not a legend.

"One in a million," or "bigger than life," those who knew Jimmy back in the old days will tell you.

But all that came to a crashing halt early on the morning of Dec. 27, 1969, when someone — using a hammer, a can opener and a knife — unspeakably ended Jimmy's colorful career in the most gruesome fashion imaginable.

And several law enforcement sources recently confirmed that the someone in question continued to walk the streets of Niagara Falls.

"Whoever did that was real demented," said George "Teeker" Poulos, owner of the Alps Restaurant and an old friend of LiBrize. "Nobody deserved to die like that."

James Anthony LiBrize fancied himself something of a Renaissance man. Born and raised in Niagara Falls, he attended Niagara University before going on to the University of Buffalo, where he earned both a law degree and a Ph.D. in philosophy.

To earn money while attending school, and maybe just for fun, there was a stint as an actor and dancer at the Palace Burlesque in Buffalo. Later in life, LiBrize was often known to sit in with the band at a favorite night spot, not doing a bad job at all of keeping up on the drums.

Opening his own law practice at the United Office Building in 1939, LiBrize quickly became known both for his oratory and his ability to win cases. Specializing in criminal defense, he was regarded as a "legal eagle" among both his colleagues and clientele.

"In court, most of Jimmy's cases got the touch of a Clarence Darrow," Mary Ognibene wrote in the old *Niagara Falls Gazette*. "He argued in the grand style and was almost sure to leave the courtroom with someone good and angry at him.

"No case seemed too small for the LiBrize touch," she added. "He could have been the poor man's Melvin Belli, or his own version of the great criminal lawyer."

The feisty attorney's social life didn't suffer, either. He was a member of the elite Century Club, as well as half a dozen other lodges and clubs around the city. Active in Republican Party politics, LiBrize once served as an aide to state Senate Majority Leader Earl Brydges. And he founded the Gourmand Club, which met regularly at the Alps.

"He was a funny guy; he had a lot of friends," Poulos said. "They'd come in, and he didn't think anything of buying a round for the house."

In one particularly humorous incident, LiBrize and his Gourmand friends are said to have bought a huge frozen octopus, which they then attempted to cook in an industrial vat set up in the basement of the Alps. The hot water revived the beast, which escaped from the vat and badly frightened a cleaning woman.

Police were called, and the octopus was shot and put back in the vat.

"What wasn't all shot up — delicious," LiBrize told friends with a wink.

But there was a dark side, too.

For all the time he spent in upscale joints like the old Alps downtown and the Century Club, LiBrize often found himself seated at the bar in one of the seedy dives along what then was called South Main Street.

And for every wealthy or

SCENE OF THE CRIME: This Niagara Street storefront, once the office of prominent local attorney Jimmy LiBrize, became a chamber of horrors on the morning of Dec. 27, 1969.

politically connected crony in his circle, there also was some down-and-outer he had defended on some sordid criminal charge.

Although he had been married to the former Cora Falcone for decades and was the father of two sons and two daughters, LiBrize was rumored to have swung both ways. Gossip about his many conquests — both male and female — was commonly circulated.

Things started to unravel in 1969. Sometime that fall, the family moved out of their fashionable Park Place residence, with Cora and the children going to a house on Ninth Street and LiBrize taking over a building at 1927 Niagara St., where he ran his law office out of a storefront while living in a small apartment in the rear.

At about 4:30 p.m. on the afternoon of Dec. 26, 1969, LiBrize met with a woman at the Niagara Street office. He cut the meeting short, telling her he was going to Lockport to handle some late cases.

"He seemed nervous, and I asked him if there was any trouble," the woman told police. "He said, 'No, my dear, no trouble.'"

LiBrize never made it to Lockport, and his whereabouts during the early evening hours are uncertain. But Robert C. Fitzsimmons, police chief at the time, told reporter John Hanchette such behavior wasn't unusual for LiBrize.

"You know, that was a favorite excuse of his to break away from someone, to tell them he had urgent business or was getting someone out of jail," he said.

Later that night, LiBrize called the woman on the phone.

"He called me just before midnight and said he was back, but I could hear a man talking very loud in the background," she told police.

Except for his killer, it was the last time anyone would hear from Jimmy LiBrize.

On the bitterly cold morning of Dec. 27, a part-time office girl LiBrize had recently hired showed up for work, letting herself into the Niagara Street storefront.

Knowing it wasn't unusual for her boss to sleep in, especially on Saturday mornings, the girl put on some coffee and went about her normal duties.

But that day, LiBrize had an early appointment in Lockport, and when it got to be 10:30 a.m., she decided to go back into his living quarters and wake him. The gore and carnage that greeted her as she entered the front room of the apartment sent her into a state of shock, and she reeled back into the office.

Hysterical and shaking, she called police.

Whoever killed Jimmy LiBrize was a sadist, there can be no doubt. He took his time in the torture slaying. In a final, fiendish touch, he neatly arranged the instruments of his atrocity — the hammer, knife and can opener — alongside the body for police to find. A trail of blood led back to the bathroom, where the killer paused to wash up after he'd finished his grisly work.

"They wanted him hurt real bad," one law enforcement source said.

The 58-year-old attorney's battered, pajama-clad body was sprawled face down on the living room floor. Blood was everywhere. It covered the floor, splashed on the walls and even spattered the ceiling. Officially, Niagara County Coroner Oscar O. Bell ruled the cause of death as "massive hemorrhages as a consequence of lacerations and a skull fracture," but that doesn't even begin to tell the story.

The attorney's throat was slashed from ear to ear, and his skull was so smashed in from repeated hammer blows that the funeral would have to be closed casket. Further mutilation was so horrific the details never were made public.

Bill Gallagher, a former Niagara Falls city councilman and veteran television journalist, was called to the scene shortly after LiBrize's body was taken away. At the time, he was a car-penter's assistant working for

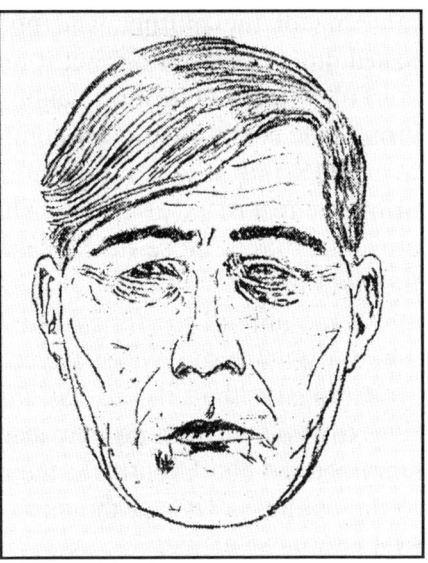

FACE OF FEAR: Police released this composite sketch of the sus-pected murderer.

the city's Parks Department, and police wanted one of the apartment doors removed as evidence.

"In the news business, I've seen a lot of unpleasant things, but nothing I've seen ever rivaled the sheer savagery of that murder scene," Gallagher said. "One thing that was really chilling, it stands out in my mind to this day, was there was a pair of boots, and they were just stuck in a pool of blood on the floor."

Police found no signs of forced entry, leading them to believe LiBrize knew his assailant. No motive was ever established, although rumors abounded. Some said it was a Mob hit, while others specu-lated it was the act of a jealous husband or lover.

One of the major problems police faced in the case was the sheer number of people LiBrize knew.

"There's hundreds," one exasperated detective said at the time. "That guy knew everybody."

And everybody knew Jimmy.

Several suspects were questioned and released. A witness reported seeing a man leaving the scene at about 3:45 a.m. on the morning of the murder, and police released a composite sketch based on his description, but it resulted in no new leads.

Following the killing, eight detectives worked on the case around the clock, eventually coming up with the man they still refer to as the prime suspect in the homicide. While they declined — on or off the record — to discuss what evidence led them to their conclusion, sources close to the case are confident they've identified the right man.

"I see him all the time," one lawman said in 2001. "Once in a while, I'll ask him, 'When are you going to talk to me?'"

Gradually, the LiBrize task force was reduced from eight detectives to two and, with no new leads to report, news coverage of the story petered out. Eventually, the investigation found itself relegated to the cold case files at the city police department and county district attorney's office.

For Niagara Falls, the dawning of the 1970s marked the beginning of a period of decline that persists to this day. One by one, the factories closed up shop and, as the jobs left town, so did the people. More than 1,000 homes and 300 businesses were torn down along Falls Street during urban renewal, and the South End never recovered. Organized crime gave way to disorganized crime with the death of Don Stefano, and even the nightclubs on Third Street were boarded up.

Murder will out, Chaucer once wrote, but in real life, it doesn't always happen that way. Barring any new developments — the possibility of DNA testing has been hinted at — law enforcement sources indicate the brutal killing of Jimmy LiBrize is likely to remain unsolved.

And the colorful attorney who fought so often to get justice for others will get none for himself.

MURDER, MAYHEM & MISOGYNY

By Mike Hudson

If you had to pick one old-time Hollywood movie star as the personification of Niagara Falls, you'd have a hard time coming up with a better candidate than the city's own native son Franchot Tone.

Scion of a wealthy family and an Academy Award also-ran, Tone was overshadowed by one wife and cuckolded by another. Tales of alcoholism, Communism, infidelity and spousal abuse persist. And his biographies contain the accounts of no fewer than three murders, including one of the most gruesome and infamous of the 20th century.

Stanislaus Franchot Tone was born Feb. 27, 1905, the son of Carborundum President Frank Tone. The family home was the Whitney Mansion on Buffalo Avenue, a stately landmark that now serves as the offices of prominent local attorney John Bartolomei.

As a child, Franchot attended Miss Otis' School, and then a boy's academy, Hill School, where he was expelled for being "a subtle influence for disorder throughout the fall term."

Using family connections, he gained admittance to Cornell University despite the fact he hadn't finished high school. He served as president of the drama club and graduated Phi Beta Kappa after just three years.

Returning to the Falls, Tone immediately incurred his father's wrath by turning down a cushy Carborundum job to take a $15-a-week acting gig with a Buffalo stock company. After a couple of years barnstorming Western New York, he headed for Greenwich Village, a community then in its heyday as a Bohemian mecca.

For the rest of the country, 1931 was a dark time. In the depths of the Depression, bread lines, soup kitchens and shanty towns inhabited by the dispossessed symbolized the national malaise.

Greenwich Village, on the other hand, was party central. A heady mix of "free love," leftist politics and nightlife, all fueled by an unending supply of bathtub gin, the Village scene afforded its denizens the opportunity to live a different kind of life, one earmarked by both idealism and excess.

Tone joined Clifford Odets, Paul Robeson, John Garfield and others at the Group Theater, a controversial troupe that later would be identified as a Communist "front" organization by Sen. Joseph McCarthy. Appearing on Broadway in three productions over the next year, Tone attracted the attention of Hollywood talent scouts.

Desperate for actors who actually could speak following the advent of the "talkies," the Tinseltown studios found an ideal prospect in Tone, whose sophisticated manner and perfect diction were the result of the upper-class background he'd rejected.

He accepted an offer from MGM. The plan was to go west for no more than a year, make a few pictures and a ton of money, and return to help bankroll his friends at the always-struggling Group Theater. But it didn't work out that way. One year turned into a lifetime during which Tone never lost the attitude that acting in films was somewhat beneath his dignity.

In 1933, while filming "Today We Live," Tone met and fell in love with a wild young actress named Joan Crawford. Best known today as the sadistic psychopath portrayed in her daughter Christina's memoir "Mommie Dearest" (NO WIRE HANGERS!), Joan Crawford was then one of the brightest stars in Hollywood.

On the rebound from her painful divorce from Douglas Fairbanks Jr., Crawford immediately was attracted to her cultured co-star.

"Thank God I'm in love again," she told a reporter. "Now I can do it for love and not my complexion."

Tone would read aloud to her from the works of Ibsen, Shakespeare and Shaw, and she would reciprocate, sharing with him her legendary sexual appetites. Biographer Shaun Considine quotes a popular Hollywood rhyme of the era, though one that undoubtedly never was uttered in Crawford's presence:

"He gave her class and she gave him ass, and Tone never went home again."

The romance, widely reported in the movie magazines, also was a boon for Tone's fledgling career. Studio mogul Louis B. Mayer — despite his own sexual relationship with Crawford — encouraged the coupling and cast the pair together in no fewer than five films over the next few years.

Franchot Tone couldn't have gotten farther away from Niagara Falls if he'd gone to the moon. He and Crawford shared a passion for booze, and their tempestuous courtship was an endless round of glamorous parties and nightclubs. But still stung by her divorce, Crawford resisted the prospect of marriage.

REEL LIFE: Franchot Tone and Joan Crawford play the role of happy newlyweds for the camera. In reality, their marriage was marred by infidelity and violence.

Until Tone met Bette Davis, that is.

In 1935, Tone was cast opposite Davis in "Dangerous." Her over-the-top performance would win her an Oscar the next year, but it was what was going on off-screen that infuriated Joan Crawford. Her bitter rival Davis was telling friends that she and Tone had fallen in love.

Three days after "Dangerous" was completed, Joan collared her boyfriend and flew to New York.

A few days after that, friends in Hollywood received word the couple had been married in New Jersey.

All in all, 1935 probably would go down as Tone's best year. In addition to his marriage and starring role in "Dangerous," he was nominated for an Academy Award for his role in "Mutiny on the Bounty," and backed up Gary Cooper in "The Lives of a Bengal Lancer," another of his best films.

The marriage, however, went to pot fairly quickly.

"Sensitive husbands don't like second billing," said Crawford of Tone, whose drinking had become worse. And columnist Ed

HAPPY HOMEWRECKER:
Franchot's fling with his co-star,
bedroom-eyed Bette Davis,
infuriated Joan Crawford.

Sullivan described the actor as a "vodka zombie." Crawford accused Tone of beating her, and often showed up at the studio with bruises that challenged the skill of the makeup artist. Both engaged in more-or-less public affairs until the couple finally divorced in 1939.

Tone's career never really recovered. Although he made 20 films over the next 10 years, with the exception of "Five Graves to Cairo" (1943), most were B pictures and his roles uninspiring.

One afternoon late in 1946 at the Formosa Cafe near MGM Studios, Tone saw something that caught his eye. Elizabeth Short, a prostitute and aspiring actress known to her friends as the "Black Dahlia," was at the bar as the actor stepped from a phone booth. Although he was married to actress Jean Wallace at the time, he found the raven-haired 22-year-old beauty irresistible.

He picked her up and took her back to the studio, where they spent the afternoon on a couch in an unoccupied office.

"She told me she'd been ill," he said later. "Something about an operation in her chest. I gave her whatever bills were in my pocket and I had the feeling that I wanted to be away from her — that I did not want to be near her.

"It was a strange and unsettling experience," he added. "Even after I called a cab for her and she was gone, the feeling stayed with me. It was almost as though I had experienced being afraid of her."

Tone would have reason to be afraid when, on Jan. 15, 1947, the Black Dahlia's nude and mutilated body was found in a vacant lot not far from the Formosa Cafe. She had been brutally tortured and finally cut in two. Tone's telephone number was found among her belongings, and he was questioned by police. The Black Dahlia murder remains unsolved to this day.

If his movie roles were uninspiring, Tone did find some inspiration in a hot little number named Barbara Payton, a blonde bombshell 22 years his junior.

The young starlet already had a reputation as a hard-drinking party girl whose steamy affairs with Howard Hughes, John Ireland and Bob Hope were widely reported. Divorced now from Jean Wallace, Tone announced his engagement to a surprised Payton at a drunken party at the Stork Club in New York City in September 1950.

MURDER MYSTERY: Franchot Tone and the Black Dahlia were two ships that passed in the night, or rather on a studio couch. Police questioned the actor following her gruesome 1947 murder.

A month later, Tone's young fiancee was called before a federal grand jury as a defense witness in the perjury trial of playboy Stanley Adams, who was suspected of murder and dope-dealing. Adams had been accused in the slaying of Abe Davidian, his partner in a million-dollar California heroin ring. Davidian had been cooperating with investigators prior to turning up dead in Fresno.

Tone sure could pick 'em.

Payton, "nervous to the point of hysteria," provided an alibi for Adams, testifying he had been with her in her apartment at the time of the murder. No one believed her, and Adams ultimately was convicted. A news photo showed Payton, clad in a mink coat, outside the Federal Building in Los Angeles accompanied by Tone and another defense witness. The resulting bad publicity hurt the careers of both stars.

And it was only going to get worse. No sooner had the Stanley Adams scandal died down than rumors were swirling of a torrid affair

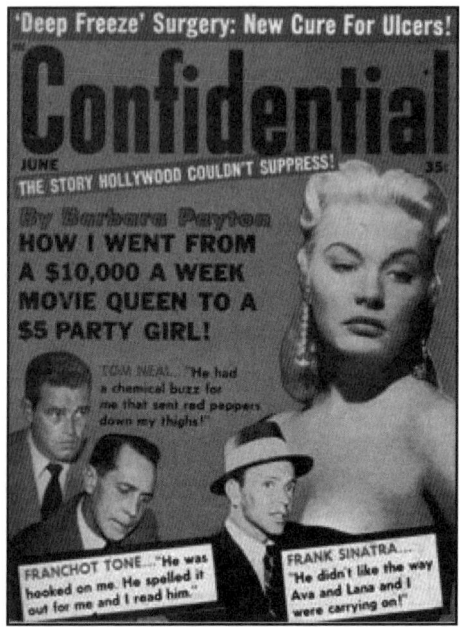

DISH DISHES DIRT: Sex bomb Barbara Payton tattled on Tone, as well as lovers Frank Sinatra and Tom Neal, in 'Confidential' magazine.

between Tone's fiancee and Gregory Peck. Tone hired a private detective to follow her.

One night, Tone barged into an apartment Payton had rented on Hollywood Boulevard to find her in bed with actor Guy Madison.

"I'm engaged to this girl and I'm going to marry her. Are you?" Tone asked angrily.

"No, I can't," a red-faced Madison replied. "I'm already married."

Payton's reaction to the confrontation was one of glee. She burst out laughing. For the first time, Tone saw an unhealthy and unattractive streak of sadism in his bride-to-be.

The incident was reported in "Confidential" magazine and brought the couple even more negative publicity. The trend would continue after Payton met and fell for rock-jawed actor Tom Neal at a Hollywood pool party while Tone was away in New York on business.

According to a contemporary article in "Exposed" magazine, she spotted the muscular and handsome Neal in the pool, "displaying his masculinity via a brief pair of bathing panties."

"The memory of whatever Tone resembled in his undies was blurred by strutting Tom's conspicuous bulges," the article added winkingly.

On Sept. 13, 1951, returning with Payton from dinner at Ciro's, Tone was confronted by Neal. An ex-college boxer, Neal tore into the 46-year-old Tone, smashing his nose and cheekbone and giving him a brain concussion. Tone would require plastic surgery to repair the damage, and newspapers across the country carried headlines of the "Love Brawl."

Things were getting so bad that many of Tone's old friends, and even his ex-wife Joan Crawford, called to warn him away from Payton. But blinded by love, he forgave his young fiancee and, just two weeks after his beating, the couple married in her hometown of Cloquet, Minn.

He should have listened. No sooner were the newlyweds back in Tinseltown than Payton launched into another affair, this time with co-star Tom Conway, the depressed and alcoholic brother of actor George Sanders, as the two were filming the improbably titled "Bride of the Gorilla." After just 53 days of marriage, Tone filed for divorce, charging extreme mental cruelty.

The couple briefly reconciled, but she couldn't shake her obsession with bad boy Tom Neal. Payton overdosed on sleeping pills in March 1952. Although Tone saved her life by forcing black coffee into her until the doctor arrived, the marriage was over.

Payton would continue to generate scandalous headlines with arrests on bad check and prostitution charges until her death of heart and liver failure at the age of 39. Tom Neal would go on to be convicted for the murder of his wife, Gale, who had been shot in the back of the head with a .45.

And for Tone, the past was catching up quickly. The scandals were bad enough, but his Communist associations with the Group Theater back in the 1930s were what really ended his career. Like many other fine actors, directors and writers, he found himself blacklisted and unable to find work.

He spent his last years appearing on television and in a few films, mostly produced in Europe. The dashing actor who looked so suave in a tuxedo, the Niagara Falls boy who went to Hollywood and made good, finally succumbed to lung cancer at the age of 63 on a warm September day in New York City.

Maybe he should have taken the job at Carborundum.

MYSTERIOUS LIGHTS
AT THE FALLS

By Mike Hudson

History can be a funny thing in that it often tells us a lot more about the people writing it than about events that may or may not have actually occurred.

Why, for example, do so many local histories include the story of Lockport's Byron Day — a two-bit burglar and horse thief who lived during the 1800s — while none include a chapter on Don Stefano Magaddino, who was for decades the most powerful organized crime boss in the country?

A little bit too recent?

Still a little bit too frightening, perhaps?

And while the tales of the dozen or so daredevils who did or did not survive their plunges over the falls are regurgitated with astonishing regularity, scant attention has been paid to the stories of literally thousands of tortured souls who have thrown themselves into the roiling waters with no thought whatsoever of coming out alive.

A bit too dark, maybe. Wouldn't want to scare the tourists.

A case in point: documented reports from the Great Northeast Power Blackout of 1965 showing UFO activity in the vicinity of the Niagara River power plants before, during and after that unprecedented event.

The basic facts of the incident are well known. At 5:16 p.m. on Nov. 9, 1965, 30 million people in eight U.S. states and the province of Ontario were suddenly plunged into darkness. Trapped in elevators, office buildings and on expressways, one-sixth of the continent's residents suddenly found themselves without electrical power.

A joint investigation into the disaster by the U.S. Federal Power Commission and the Ontario Hydro-Electric Power Commission ultimately discovered that a sudden surge of power had tripped a circuit breaker at the Sir Adam Beck generating station in Queenston, north of the falls. Line after line went down in Ontario and, by the time the surge hit New York, the charge amounted to some 1.1 million kilowatts. The chain reaction continued until the entire East Coast of the United States was blacked out.

Although experts were able to pinpoint the origin of the blackout, they were baffled by the cause of the relay malfunctions and the failure of protective systems to contain the overload. Furthermore, the origin of the sudden power surge remained a mystery.

In a Nov. 19, 1965 "Ontario Hydro Hydroscope" article, system supervising engineer Jim Harris was at a loss to explain the incident.

"It's incredible! I would have said this was impossible if I hadn't seen the evidence," he said.

Just two weeks before the blackout, on Sept. 22, 1965, in an article entitled "Many report seeing two UFOs," the *Niagara Falls Gazette* chronicled the activity near the power plants.

"Dozens of persons Tuesday night watched two unidentified flying objects moving and hovering over this area for more than an hour," the article stated. "The objects, bright lights which changed color, were below cloud level and remained at a fairly low level during most of the period they were observed.

"Observers said the objects were not helicopters or conventional aircraft. At one point, about 8 p.m., the two objects, which had been widely separated when viewed earlier, approached each other on a collision course until they 'teamed up' and moved off close together toward Buffalo," the article added.

The objects were first sighted "on the Canadian side of the river, at a point opposite Lewiston." In other words, over Queenston and the Sir Adam Beck plant.

Among the witnesses named in the article were State Trooper John Riehl, Alden residents Roselle Simon and Leonard Butler, and V.D. Price and Raymond Bright, employees of the American Standard Division in North Tonawanda.

"This was not a satellite. Satellites travel in straight lines and within a few minutes they are gone," Bright told the *Gazette*. "This hung in the sky for about half an hour. It would move off in one direction and then stop. Then it would change direction and move off again."

The relationship between the blackout and reported UFO activity wasn't lost on the scientific community.

In a statement prepared for hearings held on the blackout by the Federal Power Commission, University of Arizona physicist Dr. James McDonald contended that magnetic fields accompanying UFOs could cause sudden power surges and could, theoretically, trigger a blackout.

Writing about the event on April 2, 1968, *Gazette* reporter Joe Donaldson recalled the reports on the night of the blackout.

"After the big blackout, spokesmen for the power firms denied a strange light was spotted over the Beck Station the night of Nov. 9. Since then, however, they have admitted that sightings were reported by hundreds of people," the veteran newsman wrote.

But gradually, the "broken two-dollar switch" theory as to the cause of the disaster became the accepted version of events.

This would not mark the end of credible reports of UFOs in Niagara Falls, however.

On Aug. 4, 1966, the *Gazette* reported "bright, high-flying, fast-moving objects observed during the night and similarly described by three Niagara Falls residents."

This time, the witnesses were Mrs. George Haberle of the Parkway Apartments and 91st Street residents Russell Sorenberger and Bill Nelson. Ironically, attempts by the paper to reach Capt. Harry Meir, chief of operations and training at Niagara Falls Air Base, were unsuccessful because Meir was in Erie, Pa., investigating another UFO report.

Two Niagara Falls city policemen and a former Air Force radar chief had their own close encounters over a 48-hour period in August 1967.

According to an Aug. 25, 1967 *Gazette* article, the two officers, Patrolmen Anthony Caraglin and David Greene, saw a pair of UFOs while patrolling at 19th Street and Mackenna Avenue. They filed an official report of the incident.

"We saw two objects in the sky — one object went in an easterly direction then went northeasterly. As the object went out of sight it appeared to give off different colored lights. While the object was in sight it was a solid white light and appeared to be round.

"Object Two was the same as Object One but went from south to north and went out of sight. Both objects were in view for approximately 15 minutes and appeared to be very high," the report stated.

Howard Kay of Youngstown was working at DuPont that night. An eight-year Air Force radar chief, he told the *Gazette* the object he saw over the

SOURCE OF TROUBLE: An unknown occurrence at the Adam Beck Power Station resulted in blacking out the entire East Coast in 1965. Reports of UFO activity near Niagara Falls have been linked to the incident.

Niagara River near Buffalo Avenue looked like "an inverted cereal bowl and was lit up."

Perhaps predictably, USAF Information Officer Thomas White said he knew nothing about the UFOs.

"I have checked with the U.S. Air Force Station in Lockport, and the 763rd Radar Squadron there reports no objects logged by their radar screens at these times," he told the *Gazette*.

On April 2, 1968, no fewer than three NFPD officers reported UFOs from two separate locations.

The pulsating lights hovered for nearly an hour in the vicinity of the Beck Station, the officers said.

Patrolmen Thomas Shumway and William Wells watched the lights from Lewiston Road and Hyde Park Boulevard.

"They were like something I had never seen before," Shumway told the *Gazette*. "They were in formation and they were pulsating."

Shumway said the red, white and blue lights did not come from an airplane and were motionless until they suddenly shot away to the northwest at a tremendous rate of speed.

At the same time, Patrolman Richard Adkins confirmed the

lights were hovering across the Niagara River from the Robert Moses Power Plant and near the Beck Station. He said the lights were about 1,000 feet in the air and that, from time to time, a red streak of light would pass through the formation.

While strange lights are still occasionally reported in the Niagara skies, it appears that 1965 to 1968 represented something of a golden age for UFO sightings here.

And in the presence of so much documentation and credible testimony by trained observers, it seems difficult to deny that something was going on.

What — exactly — the mysterious objects were will likely never be known.

It is interesting to note that the U.S. Air Force employed a device to disrupt electrical power in the city of Belgrade during the 1999 Kosovo war. Could some early testing of a similar device have resulted in the 1965 blackout?

We'll have to settle for what it is. A page of Niagara history that you won't find in the history books.

THE HAUNTINGS
AT NIAGARA

By Mike and Rebecca Hudson

The ancient Celts believed Halloween night to be a time when the dead walked and all manner of sprites and demons were freed to roam the earth.

Today, it's become an unofficial holiday dedicated to children's parties and concerts by certain sorts of rock bands. But if the Celts were on to anything at all, trick-or-treaters along the Niagara Frontier would do well to make sure the footsteps they hear behind them are actually those of another Halloween reveler or, indeed, another human being at all.

Few regions in the country are as well known for number and severity of hauntings as the eastern shore of the Niagara River from the falls to Lake Ontario, the scene of countless suicides, murders and other unpleasantness down through the centuries.

Many of the legends are rooted in the lore of the Seneca Indians, who inhabited the area when European explorers first arrived on the scene. The Senecas believed the falls themselves to be the home of deities known as the Great Spirit of Thunder Waters, *He-No*, and *Lewlawala*, the Maid of the Mist.

The area around the Three Sisters Islands was said to be the location of Native American sacrifices to the Great Spirit, and sensitive visitors to the islands have reported hearing strange whispers and disembodied voices. Similarly, others have described the faraway screams and wailing of the thousands of suicides when listening intently to the roar of the waters tumbling over the mighty cataract.

Approximately four miles downriver is the 20-foot-deep cave known as Devil's Hole, said by some to be one of the most haunted places in North America. The Senecas believed it was the home of a horrifically malevolent being that took the form of a giant horned snake, an insatiable demon they called *Hanissee 'ono* — the "Evil One."

The "Jesuit Relations" of 1679 describe Devil's Hole as "a place where the Evil One and cruelty have reigned, perhaps since the Deluge."

In 1679, the French explorer Robert de la Salle ignored his guide's warnings to avoid the area. Embarking on what was to be his final expedition a short while later, he found himself plagued by bad luck, finally becoming disoriented and hopelessly lost. He was murdered by members of his own company, his body left to the wolves in the trackless wilderness.

Nearly a century later, the dark grotto was the site of the eponymous Devil's Hole Massacre, one of the most brutal episodes in the conflict known to history as the Conspiracy of Pontiac.

On Sept. 14, 1763, a convoy of British troops carrying supplies from Fort Niagara along the gorge was ambushed there and massacred by Senecas under a fierce war chief known as Farmer's Brother, who then waited in hiding for a relief column to arrive from nearby Fort Grey before launching a second horrific attack.

Screaming men threw themselves to certain death in the gorge rather than face the savage onslaught. By nightfall, the scalps of those who stood and fought decorated the lodges of the Seneca braves.

In all, nearly 100 scalped and grotesquely mutilated bodies were recovered by yet another force sent in vain to rescue them. They found dead horses and shattered supply wagons strewn down 80 feet into the rocky gorge below and the swirling rapids of the Lower Niagara River. A nearby stream still bears the name Bloody Run — a chilling reminder of the day its waters flowed crimson.

By the end of the 19th century, an electric railway line known as the Great Gorge Trolley passed by the cursed cave several times each day. On Sept. 6, 1901, President William McKinley was assassinated by the mad anarchist Leon Czolgosz at the Pan-American Exposition in Buffalo just hours after sighting the cave on his trolley ride.

Hearing the news, the Duke and Duchess of York — later to become King George V and Queen Mary — also in town for the Exposition, vehemently refused to retrace McKinley's route, riding the excursion train only on the Canadian side of the Niagara.

An avalanche of ice and snow decapitated the Great Gorge Trolley's conductor, Joseph Menzer, and killed eight passengers there on March 12, 1907; and on July 1, 1917, 12 tourists died and 24 were injured when the trolley liter-

HIGHWAY TO HELL: The Great Gorge Trolley passed by Devil's Hole and was the scene of two ghastly accidents that killed 21 people, including a conductor who was decapitated by falling ice.

ally flew from the tracks at Devil's Hole and plunged into the Niagara River below.

The official cause of the accident was a heavy rain that had undermined the rail bed. The car rolled down the steep 30-foot embankment, coming to rest on several submerged rocks before rolling onto its side and into the raging rapids. The incident was made worse by the fact that a customs officer had alerted the staff of the Great Gorge Trolley of the danger a half-hour before the accident occurred, and no action was taken. The circumstances surrounding this accident led to the closure of the railroad line a short time later, but did nothing to assuage the Evil One's insatiable hunger for human blood.

Additional violent deaths at this most baleful location have been attributed to suicide, murder and the occasional slip-and-fall "accident," and not a year goes by without another victim being claimed by Devil's Hole. Visitors tell of hearing strange, mournful voices and sighting mysterious lights in the vicinity, called by one visiting writer a place "cursed by an aura of sheer bad luck."

So common are these sad occurrences, they barely rate a paragraph or two in the local newspaper:

"Authorities believe the body recovered at 10:30 a.m. Thursday in the Niagara River Gorge at Devil's Hole State Park is that of a

CURSED CAVE: Devil's Hole has been called one of the most haunted places in the world. It has been the scene of suicides and a bloody massacre, and you can visit it today!

missing Canadian school teacher. The car of the woman, who apparently had a bad school year and was scheduled to undergo breast surgery today, was found at 10 p.m. Wednesday.

"Niagara County Coroner Steven A. Gerhardt said he is certain the woman, whose badly decomposed body was taken to Erie County Medical Center late Thursday afternoon, is the 46-year-old woman. He declined to identify the woman by name until an autopsy, which will be conducted at the medical center today, confirms her identity."

Today, the entrance to the Devil's Hole cave is 10 feet wide and eight feet high. The floor of the easterly trending passage slants gently upward, and after 12 feet the passage is only four feet high. Just past this point, the ceiling quickly reaches a height of nine feet. The passage then gradually tapers to six inches wide and six feet high in the remaining 30 feet of the cave.

Police agencies have reported feline sacrifices and other evidence of modern Satan-worshipping activity at the eerie site, but some say the Evil One, and the sheer number of tortured souls who have met violent ends there, may be more cause for concern.

A Niagara tourist guide published in 1915 expresses the sentiments still felt by many today.

"Down by Devils Hole there are mysterious apparitions, foreign language cants, and sometimes the feeling that someone is watching you or simply just brushed you gently as they passed you by," the anonymous author wrote. "The light never really does seem to shine fully on this long descent, and many locals will not go down there at night, not because of crime, because people here are very trusting. It is just a given knowledge. You don't want to go there. A few summers ago, a couple of fishermen found bones of a young Indian boy thrown down to the gorge, possibly for sacrifice."

HAUNTED HIDEAWAY: Lewiston's historic Frontier House is said to be haunted by the ghost of Capt. William Morgan, who threatened to expose the secrets of Freemasonry in 1826. He disappeared without a trace.

Just across the Robert Moses Parkway from Devil's Hole stands the beautiful campus of Niagara University, highlighted by the brooding Gothic majesty of Clet Hall, the first building erected after the college was founded as a seminary in 1860.

In 1864, a raging fire tore through the building and killed Thomas Hopkins, an underclassman who had run inside to save some personal belongings. Pleading for rescue from an upper-story window as helpless students and faculty gathered on the common below, Hopkins' pitiful cries soon turned to screams as the flames of the inferno overtook him.

"He does things, like runs around at night when people are trying to sleep," said Carl T. Tamurlin, a recent student at the university and resident of Clet. "They hear him moving in the halls, opening doors and turning on faucets and lights."

Despite their best efforts, attempts by the Vincentian priests who run the university to rid Clet Hall of Hopkins' troublemaking specter have been for naught, and many students today prefer taking their chances renting apartments in town rather than spending

HOUSE OF SPIRITS: The French Castle at Fort Niagara has been the scene of untold misery and death for three centuries.

their nights with the disturbed spirit in one of the assigned dorm rooms of Clet.

Following the river a bit farther north, the quaint village of Lewiston boasted what, until recently, may have been the only haunted McDonald's in America. The fast-food franchise was housed for years in the 1824 Frontier House, one of the region's oldest buildings and originally the westernmost stop of the Barton Stage Line. It also served in times gone by as a Masonic temple.

An Oct. 29, 1978 article in the *Niagara Falls Gazette* detailed the haunting of the landmark. Workmen involved in the renovation reported missing tools and other equipment, and the manager of the building told of seeing apparitions, hearing the opening and closing of doors or windows in the empty building, and other weirdness.

A cleaning woman described her encounters with a ghostly old man in period dress she would find in a closet or pantry, and a maintenance man quit shortly after being hired because of the disturbances. Each day, laughing children enjoyed their Happy Meals oblivious to the supernatural history of their surroundings.

The McDonald's eventually closed. Over the years, few Frontier House tenants have been known to stay for long.

The ghost is said to be that of Capt. William Morgan who, in September 1826, threatened to publish a book on the Freemasons and expose the secret rites of that most ancient order. Shortly afterward, Morgan disappeared and was never seen again.

It is said he was kidnapped and taken in a closed carriage to Lewiston, where he was bustled into a chamber at the rear of the Frontier House regularly used by the Masons as their temple. Tried, convicted and sentenced to death, he was taken early the next morning to Fort Niagara, which was at that time abandoned by the military, and imprisoned in the old French Castle until an execution party could be formed.

It didn't take long.

Bound and wearing a hooded black mask, he was dragged from the castle by three men and put into a small boat, then rowed out a short distance to a point where the Niagara River empties into Lake Ontario. Heavy chains were wrapped around his neck and, as he begged for mercy, he was thrown into the deep and swirling water, the story goes.

No body was recovered and no one was ever charged in connection with Morgan's strange disappearance. And at this late date, it's doubtful that any new evidence will surface to solve the mystery once and for all.

"Forever and forever, so mote it be," some might say.

Today, Fort Niagara and the French Castle within it represent world-class haunted attractions. No fewer than six apparitions have been sighted around the fort, including those of Morgan and the famous Headless Ghost of the Well.

As early as 1839, Samuel De Veaux wrote of the latter legend in his classic guidebook to the region. The story involves two French officers, fighting a duel in the old castle for the affections of a Seneca maiden. Her favorite was killed before her eyes and beheaded by his opponent as he lay upon the cold stone floor. The killer threw the ghastly head from the cliff overlooking the lake and dropped the lifeless corpse down the castle's 25-foot-deep well.

Legend has it that, when the moon is full, the unfortunate French officer wanders the castle looking for his lost love and the head he will never find.

Mon Dieu. And happy Halloween!

A MEDAL
FOR A MASSACRE

By Richard Hudson

Frederick E. Toy is a name revered and honored on the memorial in Main Street's Cenotaph Park for local boys who won the Medal of Honor. Toy won his as a sergeant in the Seventh Cavalry during the Indian Wars.

That's all the information engraved on the stone monument. But a trip to the library reveals a darker side to the man, as well as to our nation's history.

Sgt. Toy's medal resulted from his participation in the bloody massacre of as many as 300 men, women and children at Wounded Knee in the winter of 1890, perhaps the worst instance of butchery ever perpetrated by the U.S. Army. Currently, a nationwide movement is under way to rescind all of the 20 Medals of Honor that were handed out for that vicious slaughter.

Toy was a seasoned, 26-year veteran of the Seventh Cavalry when, along with 500 other soldiers and Indian scouts, he was sent to the Lakota Sioux camp at Wounded Knee Creek in South Dakota.

And trouble was in the air. Just a few weeks earlier, the *Nebraska State Journal* had published a story stating, "The Seventh Cavalry was itching for a fight. These are the same Indians who mercilessly shot down Custer and 300 of the Seventh Cavalry, and it is safe to say the Sioux will receive no quarter should an opportunity occur to wreak out vengeance for the blood taken at the Battle of the Little Big Horn."

Custer's last stand had taken place some 14 years earlier, but the passing time seemed to have no effect on the soldiers. There hadn't been a major pitched battle with the Plains Indians since, and the bloodthirsty throng was itching for a fight.

The night before the fateful morning of Dec. 29, 1890, the 470 soldiers and 30 Indian scouts partied with a barrel of whiskey over their glee at trapping Chief Big Foot and his band.

Before dawn, the soldiers, led by Col. James Forsyth, formed an armed square around the camp. A council of Indians assembled in front of the tent of the dying Chief Big Foot. They were immediately ordered by Forsyth to surrender all their weapons, and they complied.

But Forsyth feared that some of the Lakota men were hiding weapons and ordered a physical search of the men, as well as their tents. During the search, the troopers became agitated, lifting the skirts of the women to look for weapons and laughing, still half drunk from the night before.

The Indians became scared and confused, and within a matter of minutes all hell broke loose. Historians still can't say whether an Indian or a soldier fired first. But with that shot, every soldier surrounding the camp began discharging his weapon at a rapid pace, barely bothering to aim.

SHAMEFUL PAST: This marker commemorates Niagara Falls resident Fred E. Toy, who won a Medal of Honor for slaughtering Sioux Indians at the Wounded Knee Massacre.

The small arms fire was supplemented by the chatter of four Hotchkiss repeating cannon dug in on the hilltops overlooking the Sioux camp. The big guns were capable of firing 50 two-pound explosive shells per minute and had a devastating effect on the largely unarmed Indians.

Women picked up their babies and tried to flee, only to be gunned down by mounted troops. The men tried to defend themselves and their families, with no luck. The firepower facing them was too great. At some point, Sgt. Toy spotted two Indians fleeing from the camp and shot them both in a ravine.

Sgt. Toy was originally cited "for bravery displayed while shooting hostile Indians," but this wording was changed on the

MASSACRE: The body of Chief Big Foot lies frozen in the snow following the 1890 massacre at Wounded Knee in South Dakota.

final citation after the original was rejected by the War Department.

Capt. Winfield S. Edgerly, Sgt. Toy's commanding officer at Wounded Knee, altered the recommendation to state that Toy did "deliberately aim at and hit two Indians who had run into a ravine." Edgerly deliberately avoided mentioning the age or sex of the Indians.

When it was all over, more than 300 Indians lay dead or dying, mostly women and children. Most of the 31 troopers killed were victims of friendly fire, a result of the odd square they had formed facing each other around the camp, combined with the fact that most of the soldiers were from the east, new to the frontier and with little combat experience.

There were also some bizarre incidents reported in which a few soldiers apparently displayed some sense of morality. According to one Lakota survivor, after a soldier shouted "Remember Custer" and shot an elderly woman and then a child, one of his fellow troopers turned and shot him.

Gen. Nelson Miles, commander of the Seventh Cavalry, reviewed accounts of the so-called "battle."

"I have never heard of a more brutal, cold-blooded massacre than that at Wounded Knee," he said.

Nevertheless, Medals of Honor were handed out like candy afterward. In fact, Wounded Knee resulted in the most Medals of Honor ever awarded for one battle in the history of the Army.

And one was handed to Sgt. Frederick E. Toy on May 26, 1891. He was cited for bravery, and now stands memorialized in his hometown forever. Little in Niagara Falls is what it seems.

In 1916, Congress, acting on reports such as Miles' on Wounded Knee, decided to review all the Medals of Honor awarded in the history of the U.S. Army. By 1917, the review panel acknowledged that the medals had been given out too freely in the past, and the guidelines for awarding the Medal of Honor were greatly tightened.

In 1990, a hundred years after the massacre, the U.S. Congress finally acknowledged the grave mistake made at Wounded Knee with this apology: "It is proper and timely for the Congress of the United States to express its deep regret to the Sioux people (for the massacre)."

This meaningless act of contrition has done little to assuage the Sioux and Cheyenne whose ancestors were slaughtered wholesale that bloody morning so long ago.

Tilly Black Bear, a Lakota Sioux from the Rosebud Reservation, is leading a drive to rescind the 20 Medals of Honor given out for the action. She's asked that Americans of all races ask their congressional representatives to rescind the Wounded Knee medals.

But for now, if you happen to pass by the monument in Cenotaph Park on Main Street, look for the one name listed under the Indian Wars. It's Sgt. Fred E. Toy, hometown boy and Medal of Honor winner.

BOY SCOUT DIES
IN ELECTRIC CHAIR

By Mike Hudson

Violent youth.

Today, it's become a top priority of police departments, as teenage street gangs battle over drugs, turf and bragging rights, often armed with the latest in semi-automatic weaponry. Shootings and even murder are becoming almost commonplace in the urban environment of America's cities.

Occasionally, their ranks are joined by the lone gunman, who might kill his mother, his father or even his classmates at school for no discernible reason beyond an inner rage that one day explodes into carnage.

The psychiatric community explains incidents like these away with the "abuse excuse," most famously employed to free psychopath Billy Shrubsall following his mother's 1988 baseball-bat murder.

Conservatives like to blame our permissive society, violent movies and television shows, video games and suggestive rock lyrics. The liberals believe that additional educational and social services programs would stop these things from happening in the first place.

No one today would suggest that killer kids are simply homicidal little maniacs whose very existence the rest of us might be better off without.

Things were very different in 1934, when a scruffy bunch of kids known as the "Little Dillinger Gang" terrorized the Niagara Frontier. The gang's leaders, Bruno "Brownie" Salek, 19, and Stanley Pluzdrak, 17, went on to a bizarre sort of fame. Pluzdrak remains the youngest person ever executed by the state of New York, while Salek was the first active member of the Boy Scouts ever to die in the electric chair.

"North Enders" in Niagara Falls parlance, Salek and Pluzdrak ran a mob that included Stephan Mincon, 22, Edward Maday, 17, Alice Zimmerman, described in contemporary newspaper accounts as a "25-year-old blonde from Lockport" and John Gite, no age given, of Buffalo.

And during the summer of 1934, the gang launched an armed robbery spree in Western New York that included a dozen holdups in Niagara Falls, Lockport, North Tonawanda and Buffalo.

So brazen were the youthful bandits that they boldly held up Niagara Falls Police Department Patrolman Felix Jendrazek at the corner of 10th and

CLOSE CALL: When the infamous Little Dillingers held up the Miniature Falls in 1934, bar patrons didn't know how close they'd come to death. Stop in today and have a cold one!

East Falls streets on July 26 of that year. In addition to Jendrazek's service revolver, handcuffs, blackjack and badge, the Little Dillingers reportedly made off with $11.30 that the undoubtedly hardworking lawman had collected that day from the sale of "tickets for the police and firemen's field day."

They then hit three taverns, the Miniature Falls, which still stands on Ferry Avenue, Waldek's in North Tonawanda and O'Day's South Seas in Buffalo, in as many days. Their robberies were notable for their violence, fast automobile getaways and miserably small takes.

And when an innocent man, Albers Lepiarz of North Tonawanda, was arrested on the way to his wedding in connection with the Waldek's robbery, the Little Dillingers sent the cops a message vowing to "clip the joint off again" to show the authorities they had the wrong guy.

Things went horribly awry for the gang on Aug. 31, 1934, following the robbery of a Buffalo theater employee. The heist was snakebit from the start — the metal box the victim carried contained

TWO FALLS YOUTHS FACE MURDER, ROBBERY AND ABDUCTION CHARGES IN BUFFALO ARE CAUGHT IN OHI

Police Say Stanley Pluzdrak Named Bruno Salek as Slayer
Police Lieutenant; Arrests Follow Wrecking of Car
Stolen from Kidnaped Buffalo Man.

Niagara Falls Gazette, Sept. 4, 1934.

only tools, not the nightly receipts as the gang believed.

Two hours later, Buffalo Police Lt. George L. Uhl pulled over a black roadster containing two men after the car ran a stop sign. Suspecting them of involvement of the robbery, Uhl and his partner, Patrolman Harold Millhauser, ordered the youthful bandits out of the automobile.

Officer Millhauser began to search one of the suspects for weapons, when the other pressed a pistol against his back. The pair fled on foot and Lt. Uhl drew his revolver. Following a brief chase, the suspects turned and opened fire. Uhl went down in a hail of bullets, hit three times. He was dead before he hit the ground.

Buffalo police quickly traced the abandoned auto's license number to Sye Mincon of Niagara Falls. Just as quickly, Mincon reported the vehicle had been stolen. Mincon's son, Stephan, was picked up without incident shortly afterward at a house on Lockport Road near Hyde Park Boulevard by the NFPD and, following hours of "grilling" by Niagara Falls and Buffalo detectives, folded and gave up the rest of the gang.

The next day, wealthy Buffalo businessman Theodore B. Keating was kidnapped by two young men and a blonde woman and forced to drive to Olean.

There, he was savagely beaten and robbed of $8 and his watch by the outlaws, who left him in a cornfield, then fled in his car.

His descriptions of the assailants matched those of Stanley Pluzdrak, Bruno Salek and his girlfriend, Alice Zimmerman, now wanted for questioning in the murder of Lt. Uhl.

Even though Keating said his abductors had driven off in the direction of Pennsylvania, authorities in Buffalo weren't taking any chances. They called in the FBI and tightened security around Mincon, fearing that the Little Dillingers might try to break him out.

But the youthful desperadoes just wanted to get away. On Sept. 3, police in Circleville, Ohio, caught sight of Keating's stolen car, now at the center of a nationwide manhunt. A chase ensued and shots were fired.

Like a scene out of a 1930s gangster picture, the bandits' car crashed. Salek and his girlfriend, Alice, were injured and arrested at the scene. Pluzdrak escaped, but was apprehended a short time later while attempting to steal another car.

ONLY LAST MINUTE REPRIEVE CAN SAVE TWO FALLS YOUTHS

Governor Fails to Act on Clemency Applications; Executions Set for 11:30 P. M.

Niagara Falls Gazette, April 25, 1935.

Buffalo detectives chartered a plane and flew to Circleville to bring the trio back to justice. Pluzdrak immediately confessed to everything, and named his partner Salek as the cop-killer.

Only Alice Zimmerman showed a little class. Despite the pain of a broken shoulder suffered in the Circleville crash, she told detectives that her "Brownie" — Salek — had been "the only person to give me a break in all my life." Far from the glamorous blonde depicted in the newspapers, it turned out she had been committed to a home for the feeble-minded in Newark, N.Y., for 10 years beginning at the age of 8. In the time since her release, she had supported herself on "$3.50 a week in a Niagara Falls tourist home and almost worked myself to death," she said.

It was there that she met Salek, who later took her to Buffalo. She told police she tried to get him to go back to work as a mechanic. She said she only saw him in the daytime, "and I thought that maybe he was doing something he wasn't supposed to." Zimmerman admitted to carrying Salek's revolver, and was booked on weapons possession charges.

The murder and kidnapping case went quickly to a grand jury, which returned an indictment against Salek and Pluzdrak in an

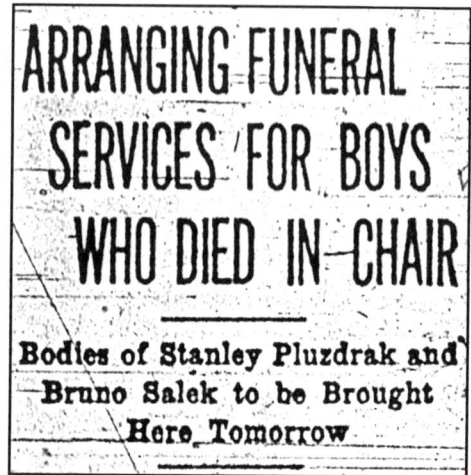

ARRANGING FUNERAL SERVICES FOR BOYS WHO DIED IN CHAIR

Bodies of Stanley Pluzdrak and Bruno Salek to be Brought Here Tomorrow

Niagara Falls Gazette, April 26, 1935.

amazing three days, thanks to the testimony of Mincon, Maday and Gite. Alice Zimmerman was standup all the way, but now even Salek and Pluzdrak were on the outs. Lawyers for the duo argued in vain for separate trials.

Salek snarled and cursed when detectives told him he would get the chair for Uhl's killing, but his iron nerve deserted him at the trial. Newspaper accounts said he was "pale, trembling and on the verge of collapse."

The Little Dillingers were finished, and Salek and Pluzdrak were convicted in the murder of Lt. Uhl, as well as the kidnapping of Theodore Keating.

Though sentenced to death, few thought the homicidal duo would be executed. They were just kids, after all. Neither one was old enough to vote.

The rest of the gang received prison sentences. Their fates are lost to history. But on April 25, 1935, less than eight months after Uhl's murder, the two boys were led to the electric chair at Sing Sing Prison in Westchester County. They both had the same thing for lunch that day, sirloin steak, and for dinner a roasted chicken.

Repeated phone calls from the prison warden to Gov. Herbert Lehman went unreturned. Albany reporters said Lehman declined comment on the case as he left the Governor's Mansion on his way to supper.

Salek and Pluzdrak died that night, between 11:30 p.m. and midnight, ushered into the hands of God, one at a time, by the Catholic prison chaplain, Rev. John McCaffrey.

Joseph Pluzdrak, Stanley's grieving father, told the papers afterward, "Just because of a moment's rash judgment, this has happened."

According to one witness, Salek had a sleepless night and "seemed some nervous" when he entered the execution chamber. Although he'd always tried to live up to the Boy Scout motto to "Be Prepared," somehow it just didn't seem to apply in this case. At the time of his death, he was just 19 years old.

For his part, the 17-year-old Pluzdrak went to the chair believing executive clemency from the governor would save his young life. But the governor never called.

Funeral services for Salek were held at St. Michael's on 24th Street. Services for Pluzdrak were held the same day at Holy Trinity on East Falls Street. In the belief that the state would not execute youngsters, neither family had made arrangements to pick the boys up on the day they were executed.

They lived as they died, though, rough and tumble. No video game or rap record was blamed for their actions. April 1935 marked the end for the Little Dillinger Gang in Niagara Falls.

And nobody missed them except their moms.

PROFESSIONAL HIT REMAINS UNSOLVED

By Mike Hudson

The old cop shook his head. "Don't even go there," he said. "Just forget about it."

I'd asked him about the 1964 murder of Sam Alaimo, a brutal crime that stunned the city and remains unsolved to this day. Of all the homicides in the Niagara Falls Police Department's cold case files, the Alaimo killing is one of the coldest.

And the old cop let me know in no uncertain terms there are people still around today who'd like to see it stay that way.

For most of the 38 years Sam Alaimo walked the face of the earth, he lived a quiet, unremarkable life. Born and raised in Niagara Falls, he graduated from Trott Vocational School and worked briefly in a chemical plant before he met and fell in love with Mary DeFazio. The couple married in 1947, and Sam took a job as a clerk at a wholesale tobacco shop owned by her father, Frank DeFazio.

Those who knew him described Sam as a homebody and devoted father of four children. But he was also an excellent businessman and, as the years passed, he worked his way up, eventually becoming president of Frank DeFazio Inc. He invested in real estate, buying a number of rental properties in his Ferry Avenue neighborhood.

When Mary began to go blind, Sam's dedication to work and family was only reinforced. His sister-in-law told the *Niagara Falls Gazette* that Sam went right home from the store every night like clockwork.

"He used to help the children with their homework and went to PTA meetings," she said. "He was not the kind of man to make enemies."

On the night of Nov. 30, 1964, Sam was helping his son with an algebra assignment when the phone rang. A man identifying himself as "Anderson" said he was interested in renting an apartment at

1447 Ferry Ave., three blocks down from the Alaimo home at 1702 Ferry.

This struck Sam as a bit odd. Although the apartment was expected to become vacant shortly, the current tenants had not yet moved out, and he had not advertised the vacancy. When he asked the caller about this, the man said he had heard about the apartment from a Pine Avenue barber who was a friend of Sam's.

Apparently satisfied, Sam told the caller he'd meet him at the apartment building in 15 minutes. But the man balked, saying he was from out of town and didn't know his way around Niagara Falls. Could they meet at the Saraceni drugstore on Pine Avenue?

Despite the fact that his car was in the shop, Sam agreed. He pulled on a sheepskin coat and boots for the walk, and left the warmth of his home for the frigid night air.

He would never return.

At 10 p.m., three young boys walking down the alley between 19th and 20th streets just north of Ferry Avenue saw what they thought was a drunk passed out, lying in the snow. On closer inspection, they saw the man's body was soaked in blood, the crimson mingling with the snow underneath. Frightened, the boys ran to the nearest telephone and called the police.

Patrolman Anthony Caraglin was the first officer to arrive at the scene. When he saw what he had on his hands, he called in the detectives, who showed up in force. Det. Bill Patti, a close friend of Sam Alaimo's, made the preliminary identification.

There are murders and there are murders, but whoever killed Sam Alaimo wanted him dead very badly. Niagara County Coroner F. Eugene Ingram cataloged 55 stab wounds, including 17 to the chest and 26 to the back that all cut cleanly through Sam's heavy sheepskin coat. There were additional wounds to the face and head, and both hands were severely cut as the victim apparently tried to shield his face from the killer's knife thrusts. Three blows to the head from a heavy object fractured the skull. The cause of death was officially listed as "internal bleeding."

"This is one of the most brutal murders ever committed in Niagara Falls," Chief of Detectives M. William Wilson told

VICTIM'S HOME: Sam Alaimo left his house at 1702 Ferry Ave. on a Monday night. On Friday, it was hung with crepe for his funeral.

reporters. "Our men are going to continue working on every possible angle in the case. We will even work at it during this weekend."

But the Alaimo case wouldn't be solved that weekend or any other.

Detectives interviewed scores of people living in the area where the body was found, and several reported hearing a gunshot at about 9:20 p.m. Dick Cobello, of 523 19th St., heard the shot, as did his wife and 3-year-old son, Robby.

"Who got shot, Mommy?" the youngster asked his mother right after the loud report.

"It sounded like a shotgun, it was so loud," Cobello told the detectives.

Police discounted the stories because Sam Alaimo hadn't been shot, but a sharp-eyed newspaper reporter, Bill Nelson, spotted something the police had missed in their examination of the murder scene — a bullet hole in the wall of the garage behind 523 19th St.

The heavy-caliber slug had gone through the side of the garage at an upward angle, about seven feet from the ground. It ricocheted off the wooden wall of the garage inside and rebounded off a pile of rolled rugs. It was found lying on the floor of the garage.

There were other clues as well. Footprints in the fresh snow in front of the Alaimo home indicated a scuffle had taken place there. One witness reported seeing a car parked in the alley in front of the garage at about the same time the shot was reported. The car turned around and went in the opposite direction.

A clerk at Saraceni Drugs on Pine Avenue said she saw a man making a call from the phone booth there at about 9:15 p.m., but could not provide police with much of a description. Was this the mysterious "Anderson" who had lured Sam Alaimo from his home that cold winter night?

Police announced robbery as the probable motive, though few people were buying it. The victim's wallet was missing, but he had loose cash in his pockets and his valuable watch and ring were untouched. Later, the wallet was recovered in a field near Gill Creek — ironically enough, across the street from police headquarters at the Public Safety Building on Ferry

UNSOLVED MURDER: This garage, fronting on an alley behind 19th Street, was where the beaten and stabbed body of Sam Alaimo, a young father of two, was found following a mob hit. Police believe it was a case of mistaken identity.

Avenue. It had apparently been thrown from a passing car and still contained $60.

Some also questioned why a robber would go to such great lengths to slaughter his victim when he could just as well hit him over the head and take the wallet.

Police thought they had a break in the case when a 24-year-old Ontario man, Robert Lloyd Anderson, told detectives he'd witnessed the stabbing. He quickly recanted his story, and later it was revealed he had a history of mental illness. He admitted he made the story up because he wanted attention and that he was "tired of just being a drunk." He was charged with giving false information to police and sentenced to 90 days in jail.

Just 10 days after the killing, Chief Wilson told reporters the case had been brought "almost to a dead end."

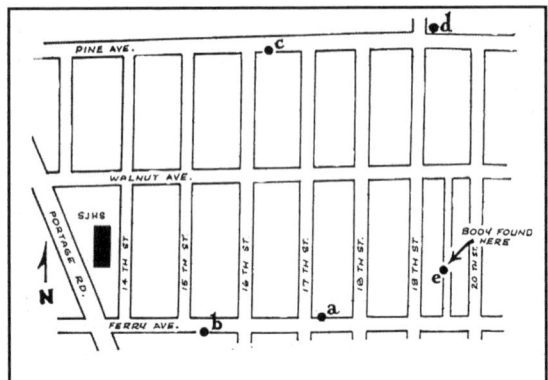

MURDER MAP: (a) Alaimo's house at 1702 Ferry Ave. (b) The apartment house he owned at 1447 Ferry Ave. (c) The Saraceni drugstore at 16th and Pine, where Alaimo was headed the night he was murdered. (d) The other Saraceni drugstore at 19th and Pine, where "Anderson" placed his call. (e) Where Alaimo's body was discovered.

Sources close to the case have reported there was a lot more going on in Niagara Falls than met the eye in 1964.

"Everybody made book in those days," one source said. "Nobody talked about it, but everybody knew about it."

Indeed. In the two weeks following Sam Alaimo's funeral at the Magaddino Memorial Chapel, state police broke up a major bookmaking operation centered in Niagara County. In all, 143 people were arrested statewide, including seven in Niagara Falls and a number of others in Lockport, the Tonawandas and Grand Island.

State Police Superintendent Arthur Cornelius Jr. said the raids capped several months of surveillance, and added that the gambling ring had an annual take "conservatively estimated at $33 million."

Cornelius declined comment, however, when asked why the police department wasn't informed about the investigation until after the raids had been carried out.

A column by Bill Nelson in the Dec. 6 edition of the *Niagara Falls Gazette* hinted at the real story behind the brutal killing of Sam Alaimo. It's a story that still makes some people nervous over 40 years later.

"Why does there seem to be an undercurrent of fear in Alaimo's neighborhood? Is it fear of the unknown or fear of reprisal that makes them unwilling to talk about what they know?

"Who is threatening possible witnesses with telephone calls in the neighborhood? Cranks or someone interested in preventing a solution to the case?"

Sources close to the investigation describe the killing as a professional hit. They believe Alaimo was abducted by at least two men in his own front yard and forced into a car, where he was savagely attacked and stabbed 55 times with a heavy-bladed knife. It was all over in a few minutes.

He was then dumped in the alley, where he apparently rallied, forcing the killers to crush his skull with repeated blows from a large-caliber handgun that went off accidentally in the process. When a witness approached the scene, walking south from Walnut Avenue, the killers turned their car around and headed east on Ferry Avenue, tossing the victim's wallet out as they approached the Hyde Park intersection.

"This was no robbery," a source said. "Someone was sending a message."

Saracini's drugstore is just a memory now, as is the DeFazio tobacco shop, where the old-timers say a lot of the business centered more on football and horses than on cigars and cigarettes.

But the murder of Sam Alaimo, the mild-mannered family man who found himself in over his head one winter night, remains as much of a mystery today as it was over four decades ago.

A SERIAL KILLER STRIKES

By Mike Hudson

It was a day when evil of the most vile and unspeakable nature roamed the streets of Niagara Falls. And before it was over, an innocent man lay dead in a pool of his own blood, the victim of a madman whose hatred would ultimately drive him to kill as many as 13 victims.

Of all the "unsolved" homicides languishing in the cold case files of the Niagara Falls Police Department, the Sept. 24, 1980 murder of Joseph Louis McCoy that sunny morning is unique, not only because the killer's identity is widely known, but because it was part of a racist rampage so shockingly violent it made headlines around the world.

By all accounts, Joe McCoy, 43, was an easygoing man, well liked in his Pierce Avenue neighborhood. Born in Evalda, Ga., he moved with his family to Niagara Falls in 1943 and attended school here. After a stint in the Air Force, he got a job as a custodian at the Niagara Community Center and attended church at St. John's AME.

Sandy Perry, then director of the community center, described him as a "gentle person, a former boxer, and the kids respected him for the help he gave them."

"Joe don't bother no one," said one female neighbor, in shock following his senseless murder.

A black man, McCoy, like many others, had been following with uneasy interest a series of killings that had begun in Buffalo a couple of days earlier.

On Monday, Sept. 22, 14-year-old Glenn Dunn was sitting in a stolen car outside a Buffalo supermarket when he was approached by a young white man, who produced a gun and shot him in the head. Buffalo police chalked the killing up to an incident of gang violence for all of 24 hours, until the next attack, on Tuesday, Sept. 23. In a near carbon copy of the Dunn slaying, 32-year-old Harold Green was shot in the head while eating his lunch in a car at a fast-food restaurant in Cheektowaga.

The case was big news in Niagara Falls, as Green's sister, Mary Tucker, was a longtime area resident who worked at the Community Mental Health Center at Memorial Medical Center. Green would linger in the hospital without regaining consciousness until he died the following Sunday.

Again, the shooter was described as a young white man.

The killer didn't wait long to claim his next victim. That very night, just hours after the Green shooting, Emanuel Thomas, 31, of Buffalo was killed by three shots to the head as he was crossing the street near his home.

QUIET NEIGHBORHOOD: The corner of Cleveland Avenue and 11th Street in Niagara Falls was a scene of horror on Sept. 24, 1980. When it was over, Joe McCoy lay dead in the street and a serial killer was on the loose.

Spent shell casings found at the scenes of all three murders showed that the same weapon, a .22-caliber semi-automatic, had been used in each. In each case the victim was black, and in each case the killer was white.

All this must have been on Joe McCoy's mind that morning as he walked north on 11th Street. As he approached Cleveland Avenue, a young white man with longish blond hair and carrying a brown paper bag "came out of nowhere," according to one witness.

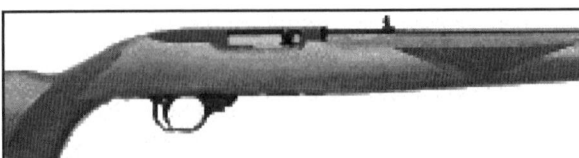

WEAPON OF CHOICE: A sawed-off Ruger .22 caliber rifle was used by the racist killer Joseph Christopher in the one-man rampage that left as many as 13 people dead. Like Charles Manson, he was hoping to start a race war.

The bag contained a .22 semi-automatic. McCoy took two shots to the head and never knew what hit him.

One witness, speaking on the condition of anonymity, said he was walking about a half block away from the scene at the time. A close friend of McCoy, he told reporters, "As I got closer, I knew who he (McCoy) was and I couldn't cross the street."

The suspect fled east along Cleveland Avenue on foot, the witness added.

NFPD Officer Ward Drew was the first policeman on the scene. He had been driving down Cleveland Avenue when he was flagged down by a passer-by.

"I just missed him," Drew told a reporter.

Four men had been fatally shot in a little more than 36 hours, and tensions rose in the black communities of Niagara Falls and Buffalo. The hysterical press dubbed the maniac the ".22-Caliber Killer." Fear escalated on the night of McCoy's murder when the body of a young black man was found in the Lower Niagara River, and Niagara County Coroner James Joyce immediately released a statement that the body was X-rayed "from head to toe," and no bullets or bullet fragments were found.

Niagara Falls Police Chief Anthony Fera Sr. urged residents to "remain calm," while at the same time acknowledging that fear was rising in the black community. City police detectives reported numerous calls from people who said they were afraid to leave their homes.

James Caldwell, a Cleveland Avenue resident, told reporters of an incident that occurred at the Airco Speer factory, where he had worked as a crane operator for eight years.

"They think they're funny," he said. "Walking around with their hand in a brown paper bag. They're just horsing around, but I'm real afraid some innocent person is going to get hurt. I see somebody come at me like that, I just might do something back. I might go to jail for hurting somebody, and all for nothing."

Bloneva Bond, a member of the Niagara Falls Board of Education, said it was the first time she'd ever been afraid in her own neighborhood.

"You can't help it," she said. "You think, who's next?"

A young black man showed up at the offices of the old *Niagara Falls Gazette* and left a note with the switchboard operator downstairs. The note was signed "Black People" and contained a warning.

"To this so-called cousin of Sam. You have killed enough of our Blackmen. We are seeking you out and will find you. And we will not be fair to you, either."

The letter referred to David Berkowitz, the convicted "Son of Sam" killer who terrorized New York City in 1977.

Community Center Director Sandy Perry said he believed the killings were racially motivated. "I think they're related to the rising economic problems in Western New York," he said. "In bad times, racist propaganda affects the least stable people. If the killer is caught before he does more damage, we may be able to contain the community. If not, I'm afraid we're going to have racial tension."

Niagara Falls police reported having to "rescue" a white man walking downtown carrying a brown paper bag with a handle sticking out of it. He had just purchased a hacksaw from a local hardware store when he was set upon by a number of black men, police said.

Black leaders publicly accused area police agencies of not doing all they could to bring the killer to justice.

It was only going to get worse.

On Oct. 8, a black taxi driver, 71-year-old Parler Edwards, was found in the trunk of his car parked in Amherst. His heart had been cut out and carried from the scene.

The next day, another black cabbie, 40-year-old Ernest Jones,

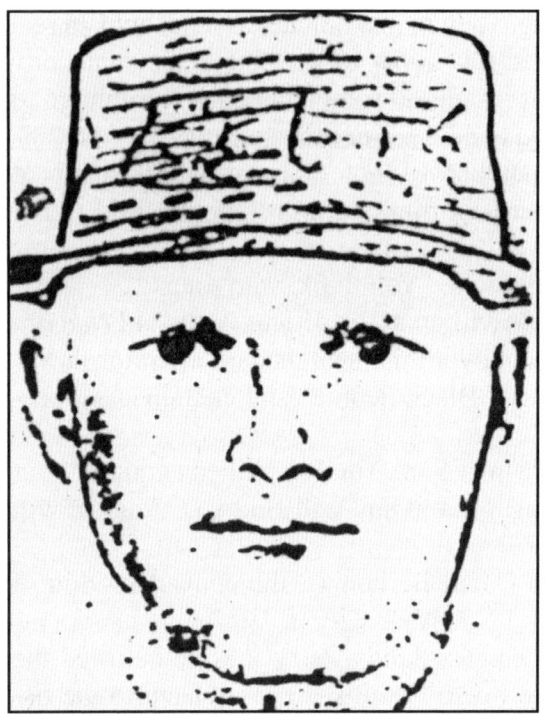

SERIAL KILLER: A police sketch of the ".22-Caliber Killer," who terrorized Niagara Falls and Buffalo in the early 1980s.

was found beside the Niagara River in Tonawanda, his heart ripped from his chest. His blood-soaked cab was found later by police, three miles away in Buffalo.

Perhaps unwisely, police began to speculate in the media that the killings were being done by a group of individuals. One did the stabbings, and two or more others did the shootings with the same gun, they guessed. In one public brouhaha, police in Niagara Falls clashed with colleagues in Cheektowaga over a proposal to hypnotize witnesses in the case.

Another attack occurred on Oct. 10 at a Buffalo hospital. A black patient, Colin Cole, was recuperating from an illness when a white stranger approached his bedside and snarled, "I hate niggers."

The arrival of a nurse saved Cole from death by strangulation, but his windpipe had been broken, and the description of the assailant matched that of the ".22-Caliber Killer."

Then things got quiet.

For the time being, no more incidents presented themselves here. But as far away as Cleveland and Rochester, the shooting deaths of black men were examined to see whether they were part of the fiendish pattern.

People questioned whether the shooting that year of National Urban League President Vernon Jordan in Fort Wayne, Ind., was connected. And at the same time, the nation was riveted by the news of the killings of 28 black children in Atlanta, Ga.

But no one was prepared for the horror to come.

On Dec. 22, in midtown Manhattan, four blacks and one Hispanic were stabbed in broad daylight on crowded city streets in less than 13 hours. All but one would die of his wounds.

Again, the killer was described by eyewitnesses as a young white man.

The horror then shifted back to Western New York. On Dec. 29, when Wendell Barnes was fatally stabbed in Rochester near the bus terminal, authorities saw a connection to the Manhattan slayings.

The next day in Buffalo, Albert Menefee survived a stab wound that nicked his heart and, on Jan. 1, 1981, Larry Little and Calvin Crippen survived separate attacks on the streets of Buffalo. All three men would later be able to identify their attacker.

On Jan. 18, 1981, a young white soldier named Joseph Christopher was arrested at Fort Benning, Ga., and charged with the slashing and stabbing of a black GI there.

A search of a hunting camp his family owned in the Southern Tier of New York state turned up a sawed-off barrel and stock from a Ruger .22-caliber semi-automatic rifle, as well as quantities of .22-caliber ammunition. The murder weapon itself was never found.

A check of Christopher's whereabouts the previous autumn showed he had enlisted in the Army at Buffalo on Nov. 13, arrived at Fort Benning six days later, and taken a leave on Dec. 19, returning Jan. 4. Cops also found a bus ticket recording his arrival in Manhattan Dec. 20. Christopher was charged in Buffalo with the Dunn, Green and Thomas murders.

In New York City, indictments were returned in two of the five stabbings.

In Niagara Falls, he wasn't charged in the murder of Joseph McCoy, despite overwhelming evidence against him. Law enforcement officials will tell you today that Christopher's Erie County convictions saved Niagara County the cost of a prosecution.

Christopher was found mentally incompetent, but the ruling

was reversed and he faced trial in April 1982. After 12 days of testimony, he was found guilty of three counts of first-degree murder and sentenced to 60 years to life in prison.

Like Charles Manson more than a decade before, Christopher's aim had been to start a race war between blacks and whites.

Unlike Manson, Christopher had very nearly succeeded.

In a 1983 interview with the *Buffalo News*, Christopher said he was a part of a larger conspiracy and claimed credit for the deaths of 13 men.

"I was ordered to kill. Who ordered me to kill? Who set up the conspiracy? I don't know," he said.

"It was just a collection of people. I can't explain it. ... I was a soldier. They drafted me and ordered me to kill. One tin soldier, you know," he continued.

The original investigators on the case have stated they doubt Christopher was responsible for the 13 murders he claimed to reporters. In particular, retired Buffalo Homicide Chief Leo J. Donovan was reluctant to attribute the two dead cabbies, whose hearts have never been found, to Christopher.

"We've never come up with any evidence that he did (kill 13 people), and he's never explained where or how," Donovan said in 1993.

That lack of closure in a number of the cases — including McCoy's — has remained troubling for many in the black community.

"That was not just an isolated incident," said Henry Louis Taylor Jr., director of the Center for Applied Public Affairs Studies at the University of Buffalo. "Those acts were symbolic of deeper tensions that still exist in Buffalo. If you don't see the connections, you don't understand the source that feeds these criminal acts."

In a 1990 interview, 10 years after the killings, Barbara Banks, publisher of the *Challenger* newspaper in Buffalo, put it more succinctly.

"This is not one thing that happened, a madman who shot some black folks and now it's over," she said. "It reminds black people there is a double standard. It reminds them of where they are. They can still be killed and not receive total justice. Some of these cases have never been solved."

Such is the status of Joe McCoy's case here in Niagara Falls.

Various authorities offered many insipid explanations for Christopher's sadistic killing spree. A New York psychiatrist said it was because he had a homosexual urge toward black men. In Buffalo, they said it was because a black man turned him in for wearing a pistol, an event that ultimately forced him to give up a prized gun collection his father had left him.

Joseph Christopher died in prison of a hopefully painful cancer in March 1993.

Ironically, one of the chief witnesses in the case against Christopher, Calvin Crippen — who survived a New Year's Day 1981 knife attack while waiting for a bus at the corner of Niagara Street and Hertel Avenue in Buffalo — was himself sentenced in 1993 on a charge of cocaine trafficking to 13 months in prison. He said at the time he didn't believe his brush with death had anything to do with his subsequent trouble.

Joseph Christopher. You can look him up on any of the Internet's many "Serial Killer" sites. His evil legacy is one of race hatred, murder and fear.

Joe McCoy. A good man and former boxer. A quiet veteran of Korea whose work with neighborhood children made him a beloved figure here in Niagara Falls.

Their paths crossed one warm September morning on a North End street corner, and only evil was left to walk away.

GHOST SHIPS OF NIAGARA

By Mike Hudson

The mighty Niagara. Fabled in song and story, both as a bucolic honeymoon destination and a cursed lovers' leap. Thirty-five miles of sometimes hypnotically wide and serene water, punctuated by the raging leviathan that is the falls, and linking the Great Lakes of Erie and Ontario — the oldest and newest of the lakes — in what seems at times to be an unholy alliance of murder, suicide and political intrigue.

Looking out at the river now, from the Youngstown or Lewiston docks, the Grand Island Bridge or the Buffalo waterfront, it is difficult to imagine that once the Niagara teemed with commercial maritime traffic. Schooners, brigs, sidewheel steamers and rum-runners of all descriptions plied these waters from the dawn of recorded civilization until the turn of the last century.

And for more than a few, the river's stony bottom became a final resting place.

Older readers will remember the April 1955 losses of both Maid of the Mist excursion boats. A fire broke out at their docks near the foot of the falls. They'd been built of wood in 1886, and had thrilled hundreds of thousands of tourists by challenging the violent and roiling waters. Their crews also earned extra money fishing out the bodies of the many falls suicides, including that of baseball Hall-of-Famer Ed Delahanty, who went over in 1903.

Subsequently, the Maid of the Mist excursion boats have been made of steel.

There was the Idle Hour, burned at Grand Island in 1901, the schooner Massasoit that wrecked on the city of Niagara Falls' water intake crib in 1904, the scow Trader, broken up in high winds at Strawberry Island in July 1908, the steamer Union, sunk near Bridgeburg, Ont., on March 18, 1928, and the tugboat Ellen O'Brien that blew up near Grand Island in 1866.

A couple of treasure ships, the French brig Frontenac and the

HMS Ontario, are said to be lying near the mouth of the Niagara in Lake Ontario and have been the target of numerous searches.

The Frontenac went down in a gale on Jan. 8, 1679.

CAROLINE

THE STEAMER CAROLINE.

UNEXPECTED JOURNEY: The steamer Caroline was set ablaze by Canadian loyalists in 1837 and cast adrift in the rapids.

Around a hundred years later, on Halloween night 1780, the Ontario was lost in a blinding snowstorm.

Each vessel reportedly carried considerable gold and silver specie for troop payments and other expenses, but the historical value of their discovery would undoubtedly far outweigh any intrinsic worth the shipwrecks might yield.

A few Niagara River shipping losses, however, tell not only their own stories but those of the Niagara Frontier during their times.

During the War of 1812, the 14-gun brig Detroit went down near Black Rock in the Niagara River. Originally built a decade earlier for the American Navy as the USS Adams, she had been surrendered by Gen. William Hull — an American commander widely recognized today as an imbecile — when he turned the whole of Michigan over to the British in August of that year.

In gratitude, the British renamed her the HMS Detroit and employed her as a raider on Lake Erie.

Following a two-month reign of terror, the Detroit put in at Black Rock, where Oct. 12, 1812, was a bad day. Lt. Elliot and a small band of U.S. Navy brigands approached the ship in a longboat, scaled her sides and took her. There's nothing recorded concerning the fate of her British crew.

There were other British warships on the river that day, and a ferocious gun-battle ensued. By all reports, the Detroit became

A WATERY GRAVE: The luxury liner Cibola mysteriously burned at dock in Lewiston on July 5, 1895.

stranded on a reef, and the tremendous pounding she was taking started a fire. She burned to the waterline.

Many Niagara Falls historians have confused this ship with a British vessel by the same name captured by Oliver Hazard Perry at the Battle of Put-in-Bay in 1813 and, decades later, set on fire and sent over the falls carrying a menagerie of exotic animals as a spectacle for tourists.

One might think that, after we beat them in two wars, our troubles with the British would be over. But that was not the case. By 1837, even some influential Canadians were pretty much disgusted with their role in an empire they viewed as morally corrupt.

One of these, a Toronto newspaper publisher named William Lyon Mackenzie, decided to do something about it. He launched a rebellion.

Mackenzie first tried to take the city of Toronto, then called York, but was beaten back and threatened with death. He pulled his remaining forces out of the metropolis, and to the south and west, to Navy Island, in the middle of the Niagara River. Here they could regroup and resupply, he thought. But such was not to be the case.

Elements in the United States, with the tacit support of expansionist President James Polk, supported the Canadian subversives. When the 71-foot sidewheel steamer Caroline docked near the present-day Power Authority intakes, on the night of Dec. 29, 1837, with a cargo of munitions bound for the insurgency, the British took action.

Under the command of Col. Sir Allan MacNab, a raiding party of some 60 Canadians seized the ship, then set her afire and cut her adrift.

While it was widely reported in the American press of the time that the doomed crew of the Caroline screamed from below decks as the flaming hulk went over the falls, it's been pretty much determined that the ship broke up in the rapids long before she reached the falls, and that the only man lost was the American night watchman, Amos Durfee. The Brits wrote a song about it, though, as they're wont to do whenever they win a minor victory.

"A Ballad of the Caroline" (published 1838) goes, in part, "The Yankees say they did invent / The steamboat first of all, sir; / But Britons, they taught their Yankee boats / To navigate the falls, sir."

So much for our "special relationship."

Another interesting shipping loss occurred more than a half-century later. The Cibola was a luxury liner mysteriously burned at her dock in Lewiston on July 5, 1895. And she was a thing of beauty. A sidewheel passenger steamer built of the finest Dalzell steel from Scotland, the 252-foot Cibola sailed from her home port of Toronto to points throughout the Great Lakes.

Specially designed for stability and speed, the Cibola was named by young Constance Cumberland of Toronto and launched on Nov. 1, 1887. The saloon was finished in solid mahogany, and the ladies' cabin presented a handsome appearance. Electric lighting, supplied by Thomas Edison, illuminated the ship throughout. A chandelier above the main staircase was made of pierced brass with jeweled openings and contained clusters of the incandescent bulbs.

At the time, the use of Edison's newfangled electric lights was thought to provide a measure of protection from fire from oil lamps, which claimed more than its share of vessels during the Great Lakes' halcyon days of the 19th century.

Lewiston, then a major seaport, welcomed the Cibola as the locals celebrated Independence Day. The cause of the blaze that sent the ship to the bottom and killed her watchman early the next morning was never determined.

Perhaps some over-patriotic Lewistonian, less than satisfied with the night's fireworks displays, took offense at the Union Jack flying from her mast and lit her up. A more ironic explanation would be a short circuit in Edison's supposedly safe electrical system.

The Detroit, Caroline and Cibola are but three of the dozens of ships lost on the Niagara over the centuries. While few rivers can match ours in terms of sheer beauty, perhaps none can lay claim to her reputation as a graveyard.

HIGH NOON IN
THE CATARACT CITY
By Mike Hudson

Niagara Falls was an exciting place to be in October of 1921. Veterans returning from the Great War found a city transformed by the availability of cheap hydropower into a great manufacturing hub, one whose factories produced everything from gunpowder and munitions to aircraft for a grateful U.S. government. The sweet smell of prosperity permeated the very air of the industrial boomtown.

On the front page of the old *Niagara Falls Gazette*, above the space reserved for the newspaper's name, a banner proclaimed the Falls to be the "FASTEST GROWING CITY IN NEW YORK STATE" as successive waves of fresh immigrants arrived from Ireland, Italy and Poland in search of steady work and the American dream.

Halloween that year came on a Monday, the kind of brisk, sunny late-autumn day that Western New Yorkers have a special fondness for. Even today, the crisp air and the falling leaves, the children heading back to school, and sunset coming earlier and earlier each night seem to give people a singular sense of excitement, the chance for one last fling before the often brutal winter descends.

Though the tourist season had ended almost two months earlier, the downtown was bustling with activity. That evening, the great Lionel Barrymore was starring in "Jim the Penman" over at the Cataract Theater, and at the Lyceum Ballroom, a gala Halloween party had been planned, featuring the toe-tapping rhythms of Brick's Supreme Syncopators.

At noon, shopgirls and secretaries joined the attorneys, doctors and other professionals on the busy sidewalks, heading to lunch at one of more than a dozen good restaurants in the district. No one paid any attention to the four men who had gotten out of a big Peerless touring car parked up the block and marched to the corner of First and Falls streets, where the Niagara Falls Trust Co. was located. Their bulky overcoats and fedoras provided little clue as to their intentions, as all the other men on the street were dressed similarly.

If anyone had looked, they'd have seen a fifth man, sitting behind the wheel of the 12-cylinder Peerless, which had been left running. But no one looked until it was too late.

There were more than 50 customers inside the bank as the four bandits walked in and pulled their guns.

"This is a stickup," the leader yelled. "Everybody over by the wall!"

He was a tall, thin man and he carried two pistols, a .32 automatic and a larger gun that some of the veterans in the crowd recognized as a German Luger.

An accomplice, shorter and fatter and carrying but one pistol and a newspaper peddler's bag, jumped the counter and began scooping up cash from the tellers' stations. The third man covered the crowd with his pistols, while the fourth stood in the doorway with a rifle he'd concealed under his coat.

George Van Auken, an architect who had called at the bank moments earlier and obtained $6,000 for a payroll, panicked and attempted to rush past the outlaws, taking a bullet in his shoulder for the trouble. Women screamed.

As Van Auken went down, Felix Woolworth, vice president of the bank, made a play for a revolver lying on the counting-room table, and the bandit leader fired three quick shots from the .32, managing to graze the banker across both cheekbones and knock him to the floor, where he remained motionless. The acrid smell of burned cordite was a portent of things to come.

Out on Falls Street, Miss Kitt Nichols, who had just exited the bank after making a deposit, heard the shooting. Spotting Niagara Falls Police Officer George Holohan standing on the rear platform of a passing streetcar, she rushed forward to warn him of the robbery. Holohan jumped off the car, drew his .38 service revolver and headed across the street toward the bank.

A shot rang out and Holohan stumbled and fell. It had been fired by the getaway driver, whose rifle barrel poked out from behind the curtained windows of the big Peerless. The driver then got out of the car and walked over to where the badly wounded officer lay, delivering a second shot as the bandit guarding the doorway stepped out and sprayed the street with covering fire.

Kitt Nichols ran west on Falls Street and was approaching the Wittigschlager jewelry story when a bullet shattered her knee. She crumpled to the pavement.

Fall Street South from Main Street, Niagara Falls, N. Y.

IDYLLIC SCENE: The sleepy intersection of Falls Street South and Main Street was shattered when a gang of bandits turned it into a shooting gallery on Halloween Day, 1921.

Another woman, Mrs. George Baker, was hit in the thigh.

"I am just so thankful the baby did not get hurt," Mrs. Baker told reporters. The fair-haired baby was her bouncing 2-year-old son, Georgie, who had been waiting with her in front of Wittigschlager's for a streetcar to her sister's place in the city's North End.

"I heard shots inside the bank and then I saw the policeman fall," she told a reporter. "A short man with a brown overcoat ran up to the policeman and shot him again through the head with a rifle. I picked up the baby and tossed him into the jewelry store door.

"Just as I picked him up, Miss Nichols, who was right beside me, fell. If I had not tossed the baby just when I did, he would have received the shot that hit Miss Nichols. He was standing between her and the man who fired the shot when I grabbed him.

"The next thing I knew, I felt a stinging in my leg and heard another shot. Just as I fell, some man, a young man whom I didn't know, grabbed me. They helped me into the jewelry store and called a doctor."

SHOTS RANG OUT: The 10th Street railroad underpass was the scene of gunplay when the Miller gang's getaway car nearly broadsided a police cruiser. Lunchtime drinkers at a nearby saloon got more excitement than they bargained for as bullets crashed through the windows.

The feisty Mrs. Baker wished nothing but bad things for the desperadoes.

"I hope they get them, for I think they were a terrible bunch of men," she said. "I do not mind my wound so much, but the thought of what might have happened to the baby and the sight of the man who shot the officer through the head, when he was down, bothers me most."

Inside the bank, the gunfire out on the street provoked anxiety among the gang. "Get that money and get it quick!" the bandit leader barked. From the time they entered the bank to the time they fled, no more than five minutes had elapsed. The newspaper bag carried by the outlaws now contained more than $12,000.

Police cars approached from Niagara Street, and all five of the desperadoes opened up with a withering fusillade to keep them back. The noise was tremendous, and gunsmoke wafted through the autumn air in pale blue clouds. Two more bystanders, a man and a woman, failed to get out of the way fast enough and fell wounded. As the outlaws made for the big Peerless, Officer Holohan rallied and managed to reel off five shots, though the massive head trauma he'd suffered affected his aim and none of the bandits was hit.

Dr. F.R. McBrien had been sitting in his car reading the paper and waiting for his wife when a bullet smashed through the windshield, narrowly missing him. Another bullet crashed through the window of Secord's Restaurant, sending patrons diving for cover. Across the street, bullets slammed into the Blair Apartments, shattering windows and leaving the elaborate Art Deco facade pockmarked with holes.

The outlaws piled into the getaway car and roared off with guns blazing in all directions. As they sped down Jefferson Avenue — now Rainbow Boulevard — a quick-thinking chauffeur named Harry Murray gave chase, speeding east along Falls Street a block to the north. At Second Street, he made a hard right, hoping to catch them in the intersection and cause a collision.

Murray's brakes locked up and he skidded off the road, narrowly missing the fleeing desperadoes, who happily sent six bullets slamming into his car. The next day, bank president George R. Shephard rewarded the brave young Irishman with a guard job at the bank. Shephard hadn't thought previously that he'd needed a guard.

The outlaws roared down Jefferson, crossed Quay Street (now John B. Daly Boulevard) and continued along Buffalo Avenue to 10th Street, where they turned left. As they approached the railroad underpass, they sent a few more rounds back in the direction of any possible pursuers or inquisitive onlookers. Bullets smashed windows at the old Niagara Inn on the corner of 10th and Buffalo, giving the lunchtime drinkers something to talk about for years to come.

Emerging from the underpass, the Peerless almost collided with a squad car racing down Erie Avenue toward the scene of the holdup. The getaway driver swerved wildly, and the bandits delivered a broadside, seriously damaging the police vehicle but leaving the two cops inside unscathed. They began a vigorous pursuit, under fire all the way, until their cruiser's engine gave up the ghost about three miles away in the town of LaSalle.

Back in the Falls, the corner of First and Falls streets became a mob scene, as curiosity-seekers gathered from throughout the city. Ambulances carted the seven wounded to St. Mary's Hospital on Sixth Street, and onlookers got a laugh when one plus-size cop slipped on a spent shell casing lying in the street and took a comic tumble. Search parties were quickly organized, one led by city police Sgt. Thomas Holohan, brother of the gravely wounded patrolman.

An all-points bulletin went out to police agencies throughout the region, but the outlaws had gotten away clean, with the same military precision shown in the bank raid.

They continued north, reloading their weapons and nervously smoking cigarettes, until the Peerless too failed, near the intersection of Lockport and Military roads. Abandoning the vehicle, they ran across the open farm fields and into Laur's Woods, a well-known deer-hunting ground of the day.

There they divided their loot, leaving the newspaper bag and the bank bands that had bound the bills scattered on the ground. They emerged from the woods and approached a farmhouse, where they found a young Polish farmer, his wife and 5-year-old son. The bandit leader told the farmer he and his men had been hunting, and asked whether they might buy some cold apple cider. When the farmer returned with the refreshments, the badmen drew their guns.

"Now hitch up your wagon and load it with hay," the bandit leader ordered. "Do what I tell you and you won't get hurt."

The young Pole was used to taking orders from men with guns, having fled his homeland when the Germans and Russians turned it into a battlefield in 1915. He'd come to America to get away from such things. When he'd completed his task, four of the bandits crawled under the hay as their leader seized the couple's son and put the sinister-looking Luger to the boy's temple.

"The cops are looking for us, and if you tell them we were here or what direction we left in, I'll kill him. Understand?"

The farmer gravely nodded his head as his wife sobbed on his shoulder. Putting the boy up on the wagon seat, the outlaw took the reins and headed off toward Tonawanda.

When the bandits arrived, the leader handed them each a card bearing the address of a fifth-floor walkup on East 59th Street in New York City, along with instructions to meet him there in two days' time. The farm boy was released unharmed as the outlaws scattered in every direction.

That night, the scene shifted to Buffalo, where detectives were questioning the man registered as the owner of the license plates used on the getaway car. He stuck with his story: The plates had been stolen early that morning, and he hadn't gotten around to reporting it yet. The man had a record.

As they were questioning him in his garage, a car pulled up with three men inside. It was after midnight, and the detectives went to see what they wanted. The car sped off as the lawmen approached.

Jumping into their own car, the detectives gave chase. After about a mile, the car was pulled over and its occupants arrested after evidence in the car seemed to link them to the bank job.

RINGLEADER: Harlan Tower, a.k.a. "Slim Miller," led a daring 1921 raid on the Niagara Falls Trust Co. here that left much of the city pockmarked with bullet holes. He was brought to justice by NFPD Det. George "Dugan" Callinan.

The next morning, Niagara Falls City Police Superintendent John Curry held a press conference. The men, Russell Battaglia of Niagara Falls, Peter Orticello of Buffalo and Fred Gravino of New York City, were being held in Buffalo due to security concerns in Niagara Falls, he said.

"Battaglia is well known to the Falls police," Curry told reporters. "He is listed as a boxer and was recently discharged from the reformatory at Mansfield, Ohio. Orticello is believed to be a former proprietor of the European Hotel, where Rola House, the Fort Niagara soldier, was last seen before he was found dying with his throat slashed several months ago."

None of the men was ever charged in the Niagara Falls Trust heist, but they remained in custody, and even Battaglia's wife, Dorothy, was picked up and jailed on suspicion.

As the arrests in Buffalo were being made, there was bad news from St. Mary's Hospital, where doctors decided not to operate on Officer Holohan. One of the bullets had penetrated too deeply into his brain, and it was decided that any attempt to remove it would mean certain death for the hero cop.

The next day, Falls residents woke to the headline "NO HOPE FOR HOLOHAN" in the morning *Gazette*.

The hard questioning of Orticello, Gravino and the Battaglias continued for weeks before it finally paid off. With the first snows of December, the investigation took a new and sudden turn.

Det. George "Dugan" Callinan was a big man whose crime-fighting exploits provided plenty of great copy for the day's news-papers. He didn't like crooks and he especially didn't like crooks who shot cops. Superintendent Curry sent Callinan to Ohio, where he located a woman who knew about the robbery, living in Cleveland's House of the Good Shepherd shelter.

The woman told Callinan that her boyfriend had recently par-ticipated in an Ashtabula, Ohio, bank job that left three policemen badly wounded following a terrific gun battle. The robbers had made their getaway on Lake Erie in a stolen yacht and netted more than $14,000 in the raid. The boyfriend had been asked to join the gang once again for the Niagara Falls heist, but declined. All of the gunplay in Ashtabula had made him a little nervous, she said.

A notorious outlaw named Slim Miller and his partner, Hoggie Reid, headed the gang and had also been responsible for the rob-bery of a fur warehouse in Buffalo a few months earlier. She told Callinan that, after the Ashtabula heist, Miller and Reid met with the rest of the gang on 59th Street in Manhattan. She gave him the address.

Slim Miller, it turned out, was an alias used by Harlan Tower, son of William Tower, the retired police chief of the nearby New York town of Kenmore. Out of respect for his family, he had adopted the Miller moniker. Buffalo police dug his photograph out of their rogues gallery, and by the next morning it stared out from the front pages of every newspaper in the region.

Callinan hopped the first train to Manhattan, where he called on an old friend, New York City Chief of Detectives Daniel Coughlin.

"I've got a live hunch on a band of bank robbers who are hiding here, Chief," he told Coughlin, "and I want a few good men to help me bring them in."

"All right, Dugan," Coughlin responded. "I'll give you the best help I can and I'll wish you good luck."

When Callinan sprang his trap, Tower and Reid were taken by surprise and captured before they could reach their guns. As the detectives broke into the bandit lair, Tower's hand was just inches away from the Luger pistol lying on the table.

"Hands up!" snapped Callinan as he led the raiders into the room.

Slowly the men raised their hands.

"Now back up against that wall," the detective said softly, and the men, chagrin and consternation showing plainly on their faces, did as he commanded them.

It was Christmas Eve, less than two months after the daring holdup, and Callinan had his men in custody.

"You know me, don't you, Slim?" he asked the bandit leader.

"Yes. You are Dugan Callinan from the Falls."

"I thought so," smiled Callinan. "Now I got the goods on you, Slim, and you had better come across with a confession. I have the dope on the Ashtabula job, and you have been indicted for that fur robbery in Buffalo.

"And I know your home address and the names of all your people," he added.

The detective then showed him a memorandum he carried, revealing the names of Tower's family.

"I see you have it all," the badman said softly before regaining his composure. "I didn't think you'd recognize me. You have the drop on me, and I guess I might just as well come clean. All I want is credit for the big jobs. I never picked the little ones."

Christmas Day broke before Callinan got the last of the confession from the men. After it was completed, he ordered a turkey dinner for the bandits.

Motorcycle Patrolman A.J. Dawson was sent to New York to accompany Callinan back to the Falls. Tower and Reid were shackled together, and Tower was handcuffed to Callinan for the trip. Dawson occupied a seat near them, riding the entire distance with both hands in his overcoat pockets and each hand gripping a revolver. Callinan's free hand was on his revolver handle most of the way, and his fingers played with the trigger.

The news that the bandits were to return drew a big crowd to the New York Central train shed at Falls and Second streets. A muffled cheer rose as Callinan stepped from the coach pulling his two prisoners after him. Dawson stood guard with revolvers drawn and walked behind the big detective as the latter marched Tower and Reid up Second to Niagara Street and into police headquarters.

"They have been well searched," Callinan told Desk Sgt. Edmond Connolly. Tower and Reid were placed in cells and, as Callinan clanked the great door on him, Tower extended his right hand and clasped the hand of the big detective.

"You outpointed and outsmarted us all the way, Dugan," Tower said. "But you treated us white."

Justice was quick in those early days, and the authorities weren't fooling around. Little more than two weeks after their return, Niagara County Judge Charles Hickey sentenced the bandits to 10-to-20 years hard labor at Auburn State Prison. He said the maximum sentence was "hardly adequate" for the crimes they'd committed.

Tower offered a terse "no comment" following the sentencing, but Reid wanted people to know he wasn't such a bad guy.

"I was up against it," he said. "I couldn't get any work, not even ditch-digging. And no red-blooded man would commit suicide. I heard of this chance to rob the Falls bank and took the chance, but I did not intend to harm anyone except in self-defense. Yes, I went through with it, but did not intend to shoot anyone unnecessarily, only to protect myself."

No one else was ever arrested in connection with the heist. Mr. and Mrs. Battaglia were quietly released from jail following the sentencing, along with their friends Orticello and Gravino. Their role in the case, if any, was never explained. Officer Holohan spent what was left of his life an invalid, and the ultimate fate of Tower and Reid has been lost to history.

Likewise, there is no record to show how the terrorized farm family made out.

Mrs. Baker had her story and Miss Nichols her limp, and the chauffeur Murray his new bank-guard job. The architect, Van Auken, never felt so confident again carrying large amounts of cash.

"I think they were a terrible bunch of men," Mrs. Baker said in the robbery's wake, and indeed they were.

A terrible bunch of men who stole some money from a bank and the innocence of an entire city.

MAD GENIUS
OF THE FALLS

By Mike Hudson

More than a half century after his death, Nikola Tesla's 265-page FBI file remains open, although copies obtained through Freedom of Information Act requests are heavily redacted for national security purposes.

His 700 patents fill a book more than two inches thick. Some of his best-known inventions include alternating current, the electric motor, neon and fluorescent lighting, the X-ray camera and remote control. When Guglielmo Marconi claimed to have invented the radio, Tesla sued him, and the U.S. Supreme Court later ruled that Marconi's "invention" infringed on more than a dozen of Tesla's prior patents.

But he also claimed to have contacted alien beings, experimented successfully with anti-gravitational devices and invented a particle beam "death ray" that could destroy enemy aircraft at distances of more than 200 miles.

Following his death, his personal papers and other effects were seized by federal agents and naval intelligence officers, never to publicly resurface despite the best efforts of members of Congress and other high government officials to find them.

Today, many seemingly outlandish theories have sprung up around Tesla, including allegations he caused the massive 1908 explosion at Tunguska, Siberia, that he was involved in the so-called "Philadelphia Experiment" shortly before his death, and even that he himself was not of this Earth.

But one thing is for certain. As a young boy growing up in Belgrade, Yugoslavia, Tesla came upon a steel engraving of the great falls of Niagara. Afterward, he dreamed of them as he slept, and even awake he lapsed into visions of the roaring waters. When finally, years later, he got the chance to visit the object of his obsession, Tesla would alter the natural wonder so profoundly that his name and that of the mighty cataract would forever be linked in history.

Nikola Tesla was born in Croatia of Serbian parents in 1856. His father, an Orthodox priest, made sure young Tesla received the best education possible, and the precocious lad excelled in his studies. At school, he was accused by the faculty of cheating because of his ability to perform integral calculus in his head. In college, he studied mechanical and electrical engineering, although he soon found that the breadth of his genius far surpassed that of any of his professors.

At the age of 24, the young engineer was working for the Central Telephone Company in Budapest, Hungary. One evening, he was walking with a friend in a city park when he noticed the beautiful sunset. A passage from Goethe's "Faust" came to mind, and he recited it out loud.

DISTURBING VISION: As a young man in Eastern Europe, Tesla had a vision that would one day lead him to Niagara Falls.

"The glow retreats, done is the day of toil;
"It yonder hastes, new fields of life exploring;
"Ah, that no wing can lift me from the soil
"Upon its track to follow, follow soaring!"

It was at that moment, Tesla would later write, that he invented the induction motor — alternating current — a technological advance that would forever change the world.

"As I uttered those inspiring words, the idea came like a flash of lightning and in an instant the truth was revealed," he wrote. "I drew with a stick on the sand the diagram shown six years later in my address before the American Institute of Electrical Engineers."

At the time, all of the electrical generating equipment in the world was based on Thomas Edison's direct current (DC) model. There were many drawbacks, the main one being that direct current cannot be transmitted more than 10 miles. Edison was in the process of convincing investors and the government to subsidize the construction of relay stations throughout New York state when Tesla left Europe to meet the inventor.

Convinced that Edison would see the advantages of alternating current (AC) — which can be grounded to prevent electrocution and transmitted over almost unlimited distances — Tesla arrived in New York City in 1881. Edison saw the new system as competition, and hired Tesla to work at his Edison Machine Works to keep an eye on him. The arrangement didn't last long. Within a few months, following a dispute over money, Tesla resigned.

After obtaining financial backing, Tesla quickly developed all of the components for the system of AC power transmission used throughout the world today.

The Faustian vision he had experienced in Budapest was now reality.

"The motors I built there were exactly as I imagined them," he said. "I made no attempt to improve the design, but merely reproduced the pictures as they appeared in my vision and the operation was always as I expected."

Tesla entered into a partnership with George Westinghouse of Pittsburgh to market the new system of power transmission. But Thomas Edison and his newly formed General Electric Company used every trick in the book to convince the public of DC's superiority.

On Aug. 6, 1890, a convicted ax murderer named William Kemmler was set to become the first man to die in the new electric chair at Auburn State Prison. Edison arranged for the illegal purchase of a used Tesla-Westinghouse generator and had it set up in the death house in order to demonstrate the danger of AC. Kemmler died horribly, in what the newspapers said was "an awful spectacle, far worse than hanging."

Three years later, Westinghouse undercut by half General Electric's $1 million bid for illuminating the Columbian Exposition in Chicago. Much of General Electric's proposed expenses related to the amount of copper wire needed to utilize DC power, illustrating the cost effectiveness of the AC system. Twenty-seven million people attended the exposition and, from that point onward, more than 80 percent of the electrical devices purchased in the United States were for alternating current.

The international Niagara Falls Commission — headed by Britain's Lord Kelvin and backed by a cabal of the world's richest men, including J.P. Morgan, Lord Rothschild and John Jacob Astor — invited proposals from experts around the world to harness the falls as a means of generating electricity.

Again, Westinghouse and Tesla's AC system won out over General

REMEMBERED TODAY: This monument to Tesla remains a popular tourist attraction on Goat Island near the brink of the American Falls. He discovered alternating current and invented the remote control, making possible much of modern life.

Electric and Edison's proposal and, late in 1893, work began on the Niagara Power Project.

For Tesla, it was the realization of a childhood obsession. Had he, as a young boy in Yugoslavia, actually prophesied his own destiny?

For the financial backers, as well as the thousands of laborers, engineers, mechanics and others working on the project, the five years spent in construction were fraught with anxiety.

Because no one except Tesla was sure it would work. In his mind, he heard the hum of the turbines, saw the inner workings of the giant dynamos. While others doubted the plant would generate enough electricity to run the streetcars in Buffalo, Tesla was confident of the falls' ability to illuminate the entire eastern United States.

Today it is difficult to imagine the magnitude of the project. At a time when most homes were lit by oil lamps or gas jets, and the horse-and-buggy was the primary mode of transportation, Tesla saw the future. His intention was nothing short of transforming the world as he knew it.

The switch was thrown at midnight on Nov. 16, 1896, sending 1,000 horsepower of electrical energy to Buffalo, now the "City of Light." Orders for more power came flooding in and, within a few years, 10 generators were running 24 hours a day. Electricity from the falls enabled New York City to become a different place, as Broadway was transformed into "The Great White Way," and the subway, elevated train and streetcar systems allowed the teeming throngs to come and go as they pleased.

Tesla's triumph at Niagara Falls sounded the death knell for Edison's DC system. By the turn of the century, even General Electric converted to AC. With success came fame, and Tesla numbered among his friends Mark Twain, composer Jan Paderewski, the naturalist John Muir and the great welterweight champion Fritzie Zivic.

The fame and fortune allowed Tesla, reclusive by nature, to leave Westinghouse and go back to his first love, research. The esoteric and arcane nature of his experiments and discoveries during the following years would provide unlimited fodder for FBI agents and conspiracy theorists for generations to come.

Tesla's researches following the construction of the Niagara power plant centered around the wireless transmission of energy. Experimenting with light, radio waves and high-frequency electrical energy, he invented the "Tesla coil," which allowed him to step up ordinary 60-cycle-per-second household current into extremely high frequencies, hundreds of thousands of cycles per second. Even small models of the coil produced extremely high voltages that allowed the inventor to produce the first neon and fluorescent lights, take the first X-ray photographs and illuminate light bulbs without wires.

In an 1898 exhibition at Madison Square Garden, Tesla frightened the crowd with the demonstration of a radio-controlled boat.

"When first shown, it created a sensation such as no other invention of mine has ever produced," he said.

The remote control he invented allowed the boat to travel about a small indoor pond at his command, and lights on the vessel blinked to answer mathematical questions put to it by members of the audience.

Some frightened onlookers believed he was controlling the boat with his mind. In a sense, he was. With astonishing speed, he mentally worked out the computations and

TESLA AT WORK: Incredible inventions. Free electricity. Time travel. Death rays. Ozone generators. Unlimited wireless power anywhere on earth. Thought machines. Radio anti-gravity airships. These were all part of Tesla's life.

used his remote-control device to direct the boat's "answers."

Today, remote controls are used in applications ranging from opening garage doors and changing television channels to guiding armed missiles and unpiloted drone aircraft. In the late 19th century, however, the concept was simply too advanced to be put to practical use.

In 1899, Tesla began construction of a laboratory near Pike's Peak in Colorado. Like something out of "Frankenstein," the lab featured a retractable roof and a wooden tower that rose 80 feet above the prairie. Atop the tower was a 142-foot metal mast supporting a huge copper globe. Inside the tower, Tesla busied his assistants in the construction of a gigantic Tesla coil with which he proposed to transmit electricity through the earth itself.

For the next nine months, cowboys and Indians in the vicinity of Colorado Springs witnessed a mad light show complete with huge arcs of blue electricity moving up and down the coil and bolts of artificial lightning shooting out of the copper globe hundreds of feet into the starry Western night.

The results of these experiments are lost to history, as the scientific notes and records pertaining to Tesla's entire time in Colorado have disappeared. Were they among the papers seized by federal agents and naval intelligence officers following the scientist's death in 1943? It was also during his Colorado period that Tesla announced he had received signals from an extraterrestrial intelligence.

Records of this discovery are also missing, although they are alluded to in the heavily redacted FBI files.

Returning to New York City, Tesla told reporters he had successfully transmitted energy over a distance of several miles, lighting bulbs simply stuck in the ground. Tesla published an article in "Century" magazine outlining in great detail the ways in which his Colorado discoveries could be used to control the weather, harness the sun's energy, cause earthquakes and alter the very fabric of the space-time continuum, allowing for both time travel and anti-gravitational devices.

With $150,000 supplied by his friend J.P. Morgan, Tesla set to work building a new laboratory at Wardenclyffe on Long Island, high on a cliff overlooking Long Island Sound.

This time, the coil tower rose 187 feet into the air and supported a 55-ton steel globe. Beneath it, a shaft sank 200 feet into the ground, and iron shafts were driven hundreds of feet below that to optimize the earth's conductive capabilities.

Tesla spent the next five years frightening the neighbors with pyrotechnic displays of man-made lightning. It was during this period, some writers have speculated, that Tesla caused the mysterious Tunguska explosion, which devastated a remote area of Siberia, approximately the size of Rhode Island, with an explosive force scientists estimate was 2,000 times greater than that of the atom bomb dropped on Hiroshima.

The true cause of the 1908 explosion is the subject of numerous scientific theories, and some unscientific ones as well. The former would include the explosion of a large comet in the atmosphere above the site or interaction with a black hole, while the latter encompasses everything from a UFO crash to Tesla, the mad scientist.

Tesla makes an intriguing suspect. A year before the blast, in a May 3, 1907 article in the *New York World*, he states that his "magnifying transmitter" had already produced 25 million horsepower, and that "a similar and much improved machine, now under construction, will make it possible to attain maximum explosive rates of over 800 million horsepower." Furthermore, he told the paper, he could direct this electrical energy "with great precision" to any point on the globe.

In 1918, Tesla developed a ray many scientists today believe to be the prototype of the laser beam. The device involved a ruby inside a globe, which was bombarded with electrical energy. The result was a "pencil thin" line of light that Tesla wrote he successfully projected onto the moon. In 1938, a headline in the New York Times proclaimed, "TESLA, AT 78, BARES NEW 'DEATH BEAM.'" The article reported that the new invention "will send concentrated beams of particles through the free air, of such tremendous energy they will bring down a fleet of 10,000 airplanes at a distance of 250 miles."

By 1937, when it was clear war would break out in Europe, Tesla sent a detailed technical paper, complete with diagrams, to a number of Allied nations, including the United States, Canada, England, France and the Soviet Union.

Titled "The New Art of Projecting Concentrated Non-Dispersive Energy Through Natural Media," the paper provided the first technical description of what is today called a charged particle beam weapon.

The Soviets showed the greatest interest, so much so that the FBI opened a file on Tesla as a possible Communist agent. In 1939, the first stage of Tesla's plan was tested in the USSR and he was paid $25,000.

It was also at this time that some say Tesla became involved in the research and development work that led to the so-called "Philadelphia Experiment," in which a Navy ship, the destroyer escort USS Eldridge, allegedly was rendered invisible through the use of a high frequency electromagnetic field in 1943.

Tesla died at the Hotel New Yorker near 40th Street and the Avenue of the Americas on Jan. 8, 1943. That's when things got weird.

According to FBI files obtained under the Freedom of Information Act in 1995, the first visitors to the dead man's room were his nephew, Sava Kosanovic, and two acquaintances. They were looking for Tesla's will, they said. They searched the room and brought in a locksmith to open Tesla's safe before leaving with a book, hotel employees who oversaw the search told the agents.

The book turned out to be a volume of greetings from prominent people wishing Tesla well on the occasion of his 75th birthday. But the FBI wasn't taking any chances. A Jan. 9 Teletype from New York to J. Edgar Hoover states that Kosanovic was "intensely disliked" by Tesla, and voiced concern about the possibility of Tesla's archives falling into the hands of the enemy.

Whether the enemy in question was Germany or the Soviet Union remains open but, later that day, agents from the office of Alien Property Control — a branch of the Justice Department — seized more than two truckloads of Tesla's belongings from both the Hotel New Yorker and the Governor Clinton Hotel, where Tesla also sometimes stayed.

On Jan. 11, a Teletype was directed from FBI headquarters to the New York field office instructing agents there to discuss the case with the district attorney's office, with an eye toward having Kosanovic picked up on a burglary charge in order to obtain anything he might have taken in his initial search of the room.

Any activities should be handled in a "most secret fashion in order to avoid any publicity in respect to Tesla's inventions," the memo states.

On Aug. 26 and 27, 1943, agents of the Naval Office of Scientific Research and Development and the Office of Naval Intelligence visited the storage facility with microfilm equipment. Following this episode, the FBI routinely replied to inquiries about Tesla's papers that the agency never had anything to do with the material.

By 1981, the Office of Alien Property — now called the Office of Foreign Litigation, Civil Division — was also denying any knowledge of Tesla's papers.

But now it wasn't just the odd researcher or fringe science fiction nut looking for the papers, it was the United States Air Force.

A 7,000-word article appeared in the May 2, 1977 issue of "Aviation Week" magazine detailing Soviet research into charged particle beam weaponry. A line drawing accompanying the article purported to depict the prototype Soviet weapon, and some analysts were stunned by the similarities to the drawings Tesla had submitted in his 1937 "Death Ray" patent application.

A curious and heavily redacted April 20, 1976 letter to FBI Director Clarence Kelly from someone in the scientific community attests to the possible significance of Tesla's later work.

Unfortunately, the name of the writer is not known, because FBI censors blacked it out in two places when declassifying it in 1980. Also withheld from the Freedom of Information Act Request were two enclosures accompanying the letter. Still, what is there is intriguing. The author states he began looking into Tesla's work in 1973.

"At the time, I discounted the possibility that these discoveries had military significance. But because of experiments now underway at Hill Air Force Base, I now suspect such military applications exist and feel it is imperative you be notified ..." he wrote.

Another series of letters were written in 1981 by Air Force Lt. Col. Allan J. MacLaren, military assistant in the Office of Strategic and Space Systems. The correspondence is written on the letterhead of the Under Secretary of Defense, Washington, D.C., and was declassified in 1993.

"We believe that certain of Tesla's papers may contain basic principles which would be of considerable value to certain ongoing research within the Department of Defense," MacLaren wrote on Feb. 9. "It would be very helpful to have access to his papers."

The FBI's response to the request has been redacted, but may be inferred by an April 1, 1981 letter from MacLaren to Roger S. Young, assistant FBI director in charge of the Office of Congressional and Public Affairs, thanking him for the effort he went to in getting Tesla's data.

Shortly after this, of course, President Ronald Reagan announced his Strategic Defense Initiative or "Star Wars" program, in which particle beam technology would be deployed to shoot down incoming nuclear missiles.

In August of 1976, a nine-foot-tall statue of a seated Tesla was unveiled on Goat Island. The FBI files contain seven pages on the event, including articles from the *Niagara Falls Gazette* and a run-down of those who attended. Cardinal Karol Wojtyla, later Pope John Paul II, was among the dignitaries who came to Niagara Falls for the dedication. Today, the monument is a popular photo opportunity for tourists, many of whom sit in Tesla's lap, mistakenly thinking he is an American president.

Nikola Tesla. Certainly he was a genius, but was he a madman as well?

The scores of books and thousands of articles written about him seem only to compound the mystery.

DANGER & HEROISM ON THE NIAGARA
By Mike Hudson

The tales of lost ships on the mighty Niagara River could fill a volume, as the remains of more than 100 are thought to litter the rocky bottom of the treacherous strait.

The British warships Victory and Boston, accidentally burned and sunk at Grand Island in 1766 and 1768, or the American squadron of 1813 — the Little Belt, Chippewa and Ariel — all lost in a fierce fight with the Royal Navy near Black Rock.

The prize schooner Detroit, taken by Oliver Hazard Perry at the Battle of Lake Erie, only to meet an ignominious end in 1841, when she was loaded up with wild animals, set ablaze and sent over the roaring cataracts as a spectacle for the tourists.

But while historians and treasure hunters work diligently to catalog these doomed vessels and record their often tragic and obscure tales, the most famous Niagara River shipwreck of all still sits today in plain view, right where she wrecked nearly a century ago.

Millions of tourists have seen her, and a large percentage of those seem to have had their cameras ready. Few today, however, remember the circumstances of her loss, or the daring rescue of her crew by the man known then as "Master Hero of Niagara" — Red Hill Sr.

She was as unloved a vessel as ever was employed on the river, a lowly sand scow that its owners — the Great Lakes Dredge and Dock Co. of Buffalo — didn't even care enough to name. In tandem with the tugboat Hassayampa, she sailed from port to port, dredging sand up from the bottom in order to improve navigation or for use in onshore construction projects.

On the afternoon of Aug. 6, 1918, she was stationed across from Point Day, near the Niagara Falls Power Co. intakes. It was 2:30 p.m. when disaster struck. The Hassayampa ran aground on an uncharted shoal and began listing badly to the starboard. Two other tugs working nearby rushed in close, one on either side of the distressed vessel, righting her and pushing her free. But the tow cable,

122 Niagara Falls Confidential

which had gone slack, now was pulled suddenly taut and snapped. The scow's two-man crew — 53-year-old James Harris of Buffalo, and Swedish sailor Gustave Lofberg, 51 — immediately saw the dangerous situation they were in. Cast adrift and with no power, there was little the men could do as the current pulled them first into the Canadian channel and then into the raging rapids, toward the brink of the great Horseshoe Falls.

"Look!" Harris screamed. "We're going over the falls! We're lost!"

But Lofberg was the real thing, a saltwater sailor who had gone to sea at the age of 16. He'd been in tight spots before. His small, sharp eyes peered keenly from his weather-beaten face. On his head he wore an old slouch hat, which he now and then pulled down farther as the wind picked up. Sweat and spray ran down his cheeks and lodged in his closely cropped gray moustache.

"Well, we've only got to die once," Lofberg replied.

Helpless, the men argued briefly and sharply about what to do. Thinking he stood a better chance going over the falls with the steel scow around him, Lofberg tied himself to one of the bulkheads with a stout rope and braced himself for the fall. Harris was all for abandoning ship, and tied himself to a wooden barrel that he planned to throw overboard at the last minute, on the thinking it might drift to the rocky riverbank, where he could be rescued. Neither plan had much to recommend it, but what choice did they have?

Suddenly, there was a sickening crunch, and the out-of-control vessel lurched forward, throwing both men to the deck. Just when all seemed lost, the scow struck a shoal of submerged rocks, becoming stuck. Their moment of elation quickly was tempered by a look at the foaming whitewater all around them. How long would it be before the wild rapids dislodged the hulk?

Looking to the north, they saw the brink of the falls barely 1,000 feet ahead.

As crowds began to gather on both the Canadian and American shorelines, the tugboat crews got as close as they dared before turning back. An emergency call went out at 4 p.m., and firefighters from Niagara Falls, N.Y., and Niagara Falls, Ont., were the first on the scene. Using a small rescue cannon, the Americans attempted to fire a line out to the stranded men, but their shots repeatedly fell short.

Hearing of the situation at the Life Saving Station at Fort Niagara, Pvt. Fred Dabney rounded up four other men and loaded an Army truck with a

RUSTING RELIC: Astonishingly, the remains of the little scow that nearly carried two men to their deaths over the falls remains today mired in the rapids, an unwilling memorial to a night of stark terror and unmatched heroism.

longer rope and a bigger gun. He raced to the scene, covering the 25 miles to the falls in an amazing 35 minutes.

The rescue crew set their gun up on the roof of the Power Station, where a successful shot was made. Lofberg pulled the line in and made it fast. Dabney then tied a heavier rope onto the light line that had been fired, and the scow's crew began the laborious process of pulling the rope in through the water and winding it onto a makeshift windlass they had fabricated.

On shore, more than 100 men were needed to keep the line taut and out of the current. The weight of the heavy rope being carried toward the falls might dislodge the scow from its precarious perch. Darkness had fallen by the time the rope was secured, and searchlights illuminated the scene.

The rescuers attempted to send a breeches buoy along the rope, but it became snagged. As discussions were held about what to do, Lofberg and Harris attempted to get some sleep. But each woke in terror when, during the night, they were stirred by some small bump or movement that might signal final disaster.

Tired of the talk, Red Hill Sr. — who had become famous six years earlier when he saved the lives of 28 tourists in what the

Niagara newspapers dubbed "The Ice Bridge Disaster" — volunteered to go out on the rope, pulling himself hand over hand until he reached the breeches buoy and could manage to get it free.

It was a dangerous mission, but if anyone could do it, Hill was the man, and the authorities gave their consent. Hanging half in and half out of the rapids, he made his first attempt at 3 a.m., but was driven back. After several tries, he managed to get the breeches buoy to the stricken craft around daybreak, returning to the shoreline hand over hand to the cheers of the waiting crowd.

Harris was a mess, and Lofberg resolved to get him to safety first. He was a family man, after all. Sometime after noon, Harris reached shore, too weak from the ordeal to walk.

By 6 p.m., 28 hours after they'd become stranded, Lofberg also made it to dry land, and the two men were put into an automobile and driven to the famous Cataract House Hotel, where hot baths and a big dinner awaited.

"I was on the barge Constitution when she broke away from the tug in the great storm of 1905 on Lake Superior," Lofberg told the assembled reporters afterward, "and for 18 hours we were tossed about in mountainous waves in the hurricane. But we weathered it then, and now we've weathered this run down the rapids and escaped the cataract. I guess I'm a lucky man." His companion vowed his seafaring days were over.

"I'm going away back on land somewhere and lash myself to a tree," Harris said weakly. "Then I'll know I'm safe."

As usual, Red Hill Sr., the "Master Hero of Niagara," allowed the men he'd rescued to grab the limelight. He would receive the Andrew Carnegie Medal for his heroic efforts and live a life of adventure on the river he loved before dying of a heart attack in 1954. His eldest son, Red Hill Jr., was killed attempting to go over the falls in a contraption made of old inner tubes in 1951, and his younger son, Wesley Hill, was credited with the rescue of more than 50 people and the recovery of more than 400 bodies from the river over the years. He passed away at the age of 76.

The loss of the Niagara barge resulted in an insurance payment of $36,000, and talk immediately turned to salvaging the wreck.

But it was believed that the winter ice floes would soon dislodge the scow and send it, finally, over the falls.

The rusting wreck hasn't budged an inch since then. A couple of years back, the Canadian parks authorities, apparently tired of answering the same questions thousands of times, put a brass plaque onshore telling the story of the near-tragedy.

Someday, perhaps, the ice and the rust will combine to knock the scow loose and send her over, fulfilling the destiny that fate had mapped. Until then, she'll stay where she is, an unintended monument to a couple of exciting days in the place known around the world as Niagara Falls.

JOHN STEDMAN:
COWARD FOR THE CROWN
By Mike Hudson

Had John Stedman been a British officer, his actions on the morning of Sept. 14, 1763, would likely have earned him a court martial for cowardice in the face of the enemy. Certainly, his military career would have been ruined and he would have returned to England in disgrace.

In one fell swoop, Stedman deserted the 25 men under his command, leaving them to be slaughtered miserably at what later came to be called the Devil's Hole Massacre. And by failing to alert the nearest garrison of British troops, he allowed a relief column of more than 80 brave British soldiers to march into the deadly ambush as well.

But Stedman wasn't an officer or a military man of any stripe, despite the fact that he was in command that day of an armed column making its way through territory known to be crawling with enemy combatants.

He was a political hack, appointed to the plum patronage position of Master of the Niagara Portage by Sir William Johnson, arguably the most powerful British official in North America at the time. And British politics, along with more than a century of fawning and incurious written history, made Stedman wealthy in his lifetime and a legend in death.

This is Western New York, after all, a place where a peculiar paucity of real heroes has often led to the canonization of more than a few villains, scoundrels and cutthroats over the years. And where the writers of what passes for history as often as not turn a blind eye to the facts in favor of civic boosterism and the nonsense of nostalgia.

Fortunately, a new breed of historian has arrived on the local scene, one not given to making a trailblazing frontiersman out of a run-of-the-mill crook. Among these is Edward W. Ahrens, who has recently brought the concepts of exhaustive original research and careful analysis to bear on the Devil's Hole fight in his excellent and highly readable "The Devil's Hole Massacre: A True Story." While he doesn't permit himself to pass any judgment, the facts presented by Ahrens provide all the evidence needed for Stedman's successful prosecution.

John Stedman came to what is now Niagara Falls in the spring of 1762 — barely a year before the disaster at Devil's Hole — to take possession of land and a fortified storehouse that had been built by two enterprising pioneers, James Sterling and John Duncan, at the end of the French and Indian War here in 1760. The men

DEVIL'S HOLE FROM BELOW.

SERENE GRANDEUR: An early engraving of Devil's Hole glorifies untamed nature while giving no hint of the relentless massacre that occurred there.

established a thriving business, transporting cargo along the portage trail from their landing on the Upper Niagara River to the Lower Landing at Lewiston and on to Fort Niagara.

Predictably, British officials didn't feel they were getting a big enough piece of the action. Duncan and Sterling were forced from the territory, and Stedman was brought in to run the business the two men had founded. The stage was now set for the catastrophe to come.

The newcomer immediately set about antagonizing the Seneca Indians living in the neighborhood, refusing to allow them on the grounds of what was now his house, as Sterling and Duncan had.

He was also niggardly in supplying the locals with rum and trade goods, and by grading the portage trail and making it passable for wagons, put a number of Senecas employed as bearers hauling cargo along the trail out of work.

While a generation of pseudo-historians has repeated old wives' tales pointing to the Seneca unemployment as the root cause of the Devil's Hole Massacre — joking about it being the first instance of labor unrest in what later became the union bastion of Niagara County — such rubbish completely ignores the big picture. In reality, the action was part of a brilliant and wide-ranging campaign organized by the great Ottawa war chief Pontiac to drive the British colonists back east of the Allegheny Mountains.

Late in 1762, Pontiac sent out war belts made of wampum to more than a dozen tribes, including the fierce Huron of the upper Great Lakes region, the Miami of Illinois, the Shawnee, Wyandot and Delaware of the Ohio country, and the Seneca of Western New York. He advocated a general uprising, timed by the phases of the moon, with the ultimate aim of completely exterminating the British army occupying the frontier.

The Seneca chief Cornplanter was especially receptive to the dark message, having sent out war belts of his own a year earlier. Despite strong Iroquois support for the British at the siege of Fort Niagara and other actions against the French in the late war, he felt his people were ill used once victory was achieved. The noble Seneca sachem pledged his support for Pontiac's campaign.

For the British, the uniting of the tribes would prove nearly fatal. Complacent following their victory over the French, fewer than 1,000 regular troops were deployed across hundreds of thousands of square miles of treacherous wilderness. Pontiac himself led the attack on Fort Detroit in May 1763, sending a signal that would result in the eruption of no fewer than 14 major pitched battles and countless lesser skirmishes over the next four months.

From the Upper Peninsula of Michigan, through southern Indiana and Ohio and deep into western Pennsylvania and the Niagara Frontier, the ill-prepared British were overwhelmed by the brilliantly conceived and flawlessly executed onslaught.

Quite obviously, it wasn't a coincidence, no mere accident, that led so many disparate Indian tribes to take to the war path at the exact same time, yet that is precisely the conclusion reached by more than a century's worth of intellectually challenged Niagara County history writers.

Labor unrest, indeed.

Cornplanter appointed a young warrior, known as Farmer's Brother to the English, as his war chief. Though lacking in any formal military training, this fierce warrior proved himself to be a remarkable tactician, and his name struck terror into the hearts of the British from Pittsburgh to Detroit.

Leading as many as 300 Seneca fighters, Farmer's Brother attacked the British forts at Presque Isle, Le Beouf and Venango — now the sites of Erie, Waterford and Venango, Pa., respectively — annihilating their tiny garrisons and putting the forts themselves to the torch.

As autumn approached, the victorious Seneca returned to their homes along the Niagara, taking the opportunity to ambush some British soldiers who had landed on the Lake Erie shoreline along the way. Once back in their villages, the warriors prepared for one last fight before settling in for the winter.

Like any self-satisfied businessman, John Stedman went about his moneymaking at Niagara Falls despite the growing threat. He rebuilt a sawmill built and abandoned under threat of British attack by the Frenchman Joncaire, planted an orchard of apple trees, and cleared a pasture on Goat Island, the largest of several islands located near the brink of Niagara Falls.

Counting on the British army to protect his mercantile interests, he permitted a garrison to be posted around his compound, and even allowed the construction of Fort Schlosser — a stockade with four bastions, a mess hall and barracks — on the property he now thought of as "his." Stedman also happily noted the construction of a fortified blockhouse at the Lower Landing, and the establishment of a shipyard on Navy Island, about four miles upriver.

All of these projects required lumber, and Stedman had the only sawmill in the district. His store could barely keep enough goods on the shelves to satisfy the needs of the soldiers, and his well-stocked tavern let no thirst go unslaked.

War-profiteering came easily to John Stedman. It also nearly cost him his life.

On the morning of Sept. 14, 1763, Stedman was leading his wagon train north following an uneventful trip taking supplies down to Fort Schlosser for shipment to the beleaguered British defenders at Detroit. Just as he approached the crest of the Lewiston Escarpment, nearly in sight of the garrison posted at the Lower Landing there, the calm of the forest was fractured by a deafening volley of close-range musketry. In an instant, a war party of more than 100 shrieking Seneca braves led by Farmer's Brother rushed the convoy with tomahawks and scalping knives drawn and sharpened.

As his men fought and died around him, Stedman had but one thought — saving his own skin. Putting spur to his horse, Stedman galloped off, leaving his command to its grim fate. But rather than making for the Lower Landing, less than three miles away, he headed for his store, a distance of more than five miles in the opposite direction. Out of pure fear, he added to the time it took to reach help by leaving the portage trail altogether and returning along the brush-choked banks of Gill Creek.

Did the men of Stedman's doomed command realize they would die at the place known to the Seneca for centuries as Devil's Hole? Probably. The lurid reputation of the place, the Seneca belief that the cave located underneath the portage trail served as a portal to the dark realm of an evil demon, would have been well known to anyone who spent any time on the Niagara. What the men couldn't know, of course, was that the creek bed above the cave, which they were crossing at the time of the attack, would be known forevermore as Bloody Run.

With the fierce Seneca onslaught in front of them and the sheer 80-foot drop of the Niagara Gorge to their rear, more than a few chose the latter and leapt to their deaths. Panicked horses and oxen plunged over the precipice, and Stedman's wagons were smashed to bits on the jagged rocks below.

At the Lower Landing, Lt. George Campbell heard the firing and set out quickly toward the sound of the guns. With him were about 80 members of the vaunted 80th Regiment of Light Armed Foot, experienced Indian-fighters trained in guerrilla tactics.

But the Stedman party had been annihilated by the time Campbell arrived, and the rescuers were greeted only by the deafening silence and the acrid smell of musket smoke that still hung in the air.

Hidden nearby, Farmer's Brother was waiting for them. Positioning his best marksmen on high ground with instructions to kill the officers first, he huddled with his main force barely 25 yards from the trail. Again he had the British where he wanted them, with their backs to the gorge.

Its leadership cut down in the opening moments of the battle, the relief column performed as feebly as had the men of the train, earning the everlasting scorn of the Seneca warriors who lived to tell the tale.

By the time the hysterical Stedman reached Fort Schlosser screaming and babbling incoherently about an ambush, most of his party and Lt. Campbell's were dead at Devil's Hole, their bodies stripped and mutilated in what was then the Native American custom. Various estimates of the number of British dead range from 80 to 100, making it the largest single defeat the Indians were to hand the British during what later became known as the Conspiracy of Pontiac.

Once Stedman regained his composure, he told the first of what would be many stories regarding his steely resolve and coolness under fire during the action. There was the painted Seneca brave who attempted to stop his escape by grabbing the horse's reins, only to be foiled by the quick-thinking Stedman, who cut the reins with his saber. In another version, the reins had been shot away by a Seneca musket ball fired at point-blank range.

He took no responsibility for his actions, going so far as to state that his hasty exit from the field of battle was motivated out of concern for the garrison at Fort Schlosser, which may have been in danger of getting overrun as well.

Stedman even had the chutzpah to seek damages from the British government for the financial loss he suffered as a result of the attack. He was ultimately relieved of his portage-master duties, but managed to insinuate himself back in when his successor was called up for active duty during the Revolutionary War and killed while fighting the American colonists.

Ironically, as Stedman worked for the British during the Revolution, his nemesis at Devil's Hole, Farmer's Brother, helped the American cause. Even past the age of 70, Farmer's Brother served the Americans bravely in the War of 1812, and was buried in Buffalo with full military honors following his death in 1815.

A wealthy man, Stedman retired to England to lead the dissolute life of a peer. But despite the ill-gotten fortune he made running the portage business Sterling and Duncan had founded, and the sawmill first operated by the Frenchman Joncaire, he still wasn't satisfied.

Stedman continued to pursue land claims against the American government until his death in 1808, arguing he was given title to all the land from Devil's Hole to Fort Schlosser by the Senecas as an apology for trying to kill a man made invincible by the obvious protection of a supernatural deity.

The truly bad "local historians" will continue to publish their pamphlets and pass them off to tourists looking for something to keep the children occupied on the way home. The kids will read tall tales about Stedman's warm-and-fuzzy side — Goat Island was named by Stedman to celebrate the survival of a goat left alone there one winter — or the plucky drummer boy of Devil's Hole, William Mathews, who jumped over the cliff in terror and was saved when his drum straps became caught on a tree.

"Legend has it ..." is the poor dodge meant to take the place of solid research and a keen understanding of the subject matter.

Rather than the gallant frontiersman portrayed by the pamphleteers, Stedman was, in fact, a corrupt coward, an opportunist, liar and war profiteer who was willing to sacrifice anyone and anything that got in the way of his own self-interest.

So save the fairy tales for the kiddies. When it comes to history, I'll take mine straight.

LOST TREASURE AT BURNT SHIP BAY

By Mike Hudson

It was July 23, 1759, and the plight of the French garrison at Fort Niagara grew more desperate by the hour. For 19 days, the fort had been under constant bombardment by the siege guns of an army of nearly 2,500 men — British soldiers and their Mohawk allies — then under the command of Sir William Johnson.

There was little the 486 French defenders could do as the British pounded the fort with heavy cannon fire and engineers worked night and day digging long trenches that brought the big guns ever closer to the crumbling walls of the citadel. As supplies of food and ammunition neared exhaustion, Niagara's French commander, Capt. Pierre Pouchot, had no way of knowing whether the reinforcements he'd sent for more than a month earlier were on their way.

But as night fell, the French relief column was indeed on its way, less than a mile to the south, making camp for the night near the Niagara River near a broad meadow known as La Belle Famille, the site of the present-day village of Youngstown. Numbering around 900 men and made up of French regulars, Canadian militia and Delaware and Huron warriors enlisted from the Ohio country, the force was tasked with breaking through the siege lines and driving the British back east along the Lake Ontario shoreline.

It was a bold plan and it might have even worked had not a Mohawk scouting party already discovered the French column and returned to Fort Niagara to sound the alarm. After hearing their report, Johnson wasted no time in assembling his own fighting force. Rather than waiting for an attack, he would meet the enemy on his terms.

By the morning of July 24, Johnson had positioned his Mohawk and Canadian fighters on the French flanks, while the main British force, handpicked regulars chosen for their experience in frontier combat, assembled directly to the front of the enemy encampment.

MUTE MONUMENT: The old stone chimney stands neglected near a vacant downtown lot.

At the first light of dawn, as the French assembled into attack formation, Johnson gave the signal, and a heavy ambuscade of musket balls and arrows came raining down from the tree lines to the right and left. Sir William didn't wait for a second volley and led his main force in a wild bayonet charge, plunging cold steel into the heart of the panicking French.

Excited at the sight of Johnson's heroics, the Mohawks rushed to join the fray, and to the accompaniment of blood-curdling war cries put their tomahawks and scalping knives to good service. The French line disintegrated as terrified soldiers dropped their muskets and ran for their lives.

Fifteen minutes later, the battle was over and nearly 300 of the French force were killed or captured. Among the latter was the expedition's commander, Col. D'Aubrey Ligneris, who watched in anguish as the Mohawks — along with the Delaware and Huron warriors he himself had brought — joined in savage pursuit of what remained of his shattered column.

They chased the fleeing French south along the 16-mile portage trail bypassing the thunderous falls and connecting the upper and lower branches of the Niagara River. Those who weren't overtaken and killed in the running battle stopped at their landing place long enough to put the torch to the wooden blockhouses and palisade walls of Fort du Portage, lest that outpost too fall into British hands.

Today, the fort's old stone chimney still stands in a vacant lot near the Seneca casino in downtown Niagara Falls.

Exhausted and fearful that the main British army would be upon them at any minute, the beleaguered survivors boarded the bateaux that had delivered them to the scene of their disaster and began rowing upriver for all they were worth.

They needn't have worried. Knowing they were finished as a fighting force, Johnson no longer had any interest in them. He left the field at La Belle Famille and returned to Fort Niagara, where he allowed some of the prisoners to be freed and enter the fort. Negotiations for surrender began immediately once Capt. Pouchot realized that no help would arrive, and the French garrison formally capitulated the next day.

But it is with the survivors — and the legend of their treasure — that we are concerned. Four miles above the falls, in the center of the Niagara River, lies Grand Island, which the French had used as a staging point for their doomed attack. A small deepwater inlet at the island's north end had been used as an anchorage for the fleet of flat-bottomed bateaux and two larger vessels that transported the French force from Fort Presque Isle — the site of present-day Erie, Pa. — across the eastern shoreline of Lake Erie to the mouth of the Niagara at what is now Buffalo.

While historians have debated about the makeup of this French fleet, it was certainly large enough to accommodate 900 fighters, along with enough supplies to last them on the 250-mile voyage from Detroit to Niagara, and the munitions required to defeat an army once they'd arrived. The largest bateaux of the era were up to 58 feet in length and could carry as much as 10 tons of cargo.

Sieur Claireaux, who had taken charge of the shattered French expedition, still didn't know of Johnson's intentions, but the fleet he now commanded could wreak all manner of havoc on Lake Erie should it fall into British hands. Seaborne assaults on the French strongholds of Presque Isle and Detroit seemed the logical next steps now that Fort Niagara had fallen.

And so, before vanishing with his men into the mists of time, Claireaux ordered most of the bateaux and whatever vessels he commanded burned at their moorings, leaving behind an enduring mystery.

At eight miles long by six in width, Grand Island is the largest inland island in the United States. Its modern-day shoreline dotted with marinas, parks, a public golf course and a private country club, the island now serves as a bedroom community for families whose incomes derive from the far more urban surroundings of the near-by cities of Buffalo and Niagara Falls.

But it's doubtful that many of the 19,000 upwardly mobile young professionals who live there today have ever heard of the legend of Burnt Ship Bay or of the fabulous treasure said to have been buried there by the French.

The existence of the hidden French hoard became known almost immediately following the surrender of Fort Niagara, as the Ohio Indians who'd accompanied the French got to know their newfound Mohawk friends over tankards of rum. In fact, reports of the treasure were appearing in newspapers back east less than a month later.

One article on the battle, in the Aug. 23, 1759 issue of the *Maryland Gazette*, states, "By a letter from Niagara of the 21st ult., we learn that by the assistance and influence of Sir William Johnson there were upwards of eleven hundred Indians convened there, who by their good behavior have justly gained the esteem of the whole army; and that Sir William, being informed that the enemy had buried a quantity of goods on an island about twenty miles from the post, sent a number of Indians to search for them."

While the Indians returned with a quantity of beaver pelts and other furs, no treasure was found, and the search was eventually called off.

Later, American colonists, noting the blackened wreckage beneath the clear water of the inlet, dubbed it Burnt Ship Bay, often salvaging chain, bits of iron and lead shot from the rotting hulks. A June 22, 1825 article on the Niagara region in the *Ontario Repository* mentions the site: "At the north end of Grand Island and almost in view of the Falls of Niagara, is a small bay, called Burnt Ship Bay, which takes its name from the hulks of several vessels sunk on that spot during the old French War; and tradition says they were sunk with all their military chests and munitions of war, fearing the enemy coming so sudden upon them, as to leave no time to escape."

Talk of the scuttled ships and buried French treasure continued, even as the spot became popular with anglers for the schools of perch and bass the tangled wreckage attracted.

It wasn't hard for the fishermen to find. As late as 1864 and 1866, the botanist George W. Clinton and the Hon. Lewis F. Allen each wrote in their journals of being able to see the broken mast-heads of at least one of the ships protruding a few inches above the water.

Often referred to as "frigates," it is likely that the vessels that gave Burnt Ship Bay its name were of smaller configuration, perhaps simply gunboats, lateen-rigged gundalows then in common use, or even glorified sail-rigged bateaux themselves. Of the nine vessels listed as lost by the French during the war, surviving records contain identification for only two, and both of these were lost on Lake Ontario, where the British squadron posed a significant naval threat.

While the British had no ships on Lake Erie, the French were far more active there, and colonial-era French coins have been recovered for years by divers from an ancient wreck off Erie, Pa.

Harry M. DeBan, chief historian at Fort Niagara today, has convincingly argued that two British warships, the Victory and the Boston, were accidentally burned and sunk at Grand Island in 1766 and 1768, and he believes these are the wrecks noted by later observers. But until scientific explorations are conducted on the bottom of Burnt Ship Bay, the matter remains open to conjecture.

Born in 1890, the late Reginald P. Long was once the resident expert on Grand Island history in general and the treasure of Burnt Ship Bay in particular.

"My grandfather told me about a couple of men who came over here one time from Tonawanda," Long told *Buffalo Magazine* in a 1967 interview. "They gave him $5 for the use of his wagon and also to help them dig. He showed them Burnt Ship Creek and they got out some kind of a map and asked him if that tree over there was black walnut. He said it was and they started measuring distances. After measuring, they began digging.

"The reason I remember the story is my grandfather used to take me up there and show me the hole left by all the digging," he added.

Long's grandfather also recalled the famous "Blizzard of '88," which dumped four and five feet of snow on Boston, New York City and Philadelphia, completely shutting down the northeast coast and causing hundreds of deaths. While the Niagara region escaped the snowfall, hurricane-force winds buffeted the area during the storm.

At Burnt Ship Bay, the high winds exposed a mysterious circular stone foundation near the water's edge, and residents recovered a number of gold and silver coins, the earliest dated 1537. In his classic "Myths & Legends of Our Own Land," Charles M. Skinner theorizes that the foundation was that of an early French trading post documented by the Jesuits.

"The house is not far from the water, as ships used to unload cargo there, and it is believed a number of chests are buried nearby," Skinner wrote.

As with the identities of the ships resting at the bottom of Burnt Ship Bay, the value and composition of the treasure buried there must also be deduced. We have the hard evidence of gold and silver specie being recovered, perhaps part of a payroll sent to ease the burden of Fort Niagara's defenders after enduring a siege lasting more than two months.

Also likely would be a large quantity of Indian trade goods, both as a reward for the Huron and Delaware warriors who'd accompanied the relief column and as an enticement for Johnson's Mohawk allies to align themselves with the French. These goods would range from prosaic items such as glass beads, iron axes, knives, kettles and arrow points, to the highly prized silver jewelry the French were renowned for among the Indians on the frontier. Thousands of French silver medals, gorgets, armbands, earrings and the well-known Jesuit crosses have been recovered by archeologists working on both sides of the Niagara River. Today, private collectors and museums pay fantastic sums for these historically significant works of the silversmith's art.

One day perhaps, the many legends surrounding Burnt Ship Bay will be unraveled. Maybe by a child walking along the beach, or a utility worker laying an underground cable. Or maybe by an amateur treasure hunter who's done his homework and come equipped with the latest in electronic detection gear.

When — if — that happens, the final chapter can be written on one of the region's most enduring mysteries, that of a fabulous treasure lost almost 250 years ago. What an ending that would be.

MURDER IN
THE MUSEUM
By Mike Hudson

On a farm outside of East Liverpool, Ohio, Pretty Boy Floyd had been gunned down by a squad of federal agents led by the most famous G-man of them all, Melvin Purvis. The dapper desperado had enjoyed dinner at the home of Ellen Conkle, paid her a dollar and left by a rear window in a vain effort to elude the men who would kill him.

The news came over the radio that morning, and the whole town was talking about it. But by the time the old *Niagara Falls Gazette* came out late that afternoon, the talk had turned to crime of a more local nature.

Harry "The Whiz" White had fought 36 fights during the 1920s, ending his career as a lightweight with a record of 20-10-6 and a quintessential Irish face that hadn't been mauled too badly. He'd had a few money bouts, most notably a lost decision to the Canadian champion Tommy Mitchell in 1923, and managed to save enough to buy a home outside of town in what was then known as Wheatfield Farms, where he lived with his wife and two sons.

Early on the morning of Oct. 23, 1934, he was tending bar at the Museum Grill, a bar, restaurant and gambling den owned by a Jewish gangster named Moe Schwartz, who led a small, mixed mob of Irish and Jewish toughs out of the place.

Harry White fit right in. He was fond of a drink and could turn on the charm like nobody's business. But beneath it all lay a black streak and fearlessness that made him a dangerous man.

His last professional fight had been back in 1926 against heavyweight contender Harry Wine, "The Fighting Blacksmith" of Roundup, Mt. White lost by a knockout in the third round of the scheduled four-rounder, but not before making things very interesting for his much larger opponent.

Things had been quiet for most of the night. As usual, the Museum Grill had stayed open far past closing time, a tip of the hat from graveyard shift Capt. Patrick J. Carmody, Chief of Detectives Martin Considine and beat Det. Robert Fitzsimmons. One thing about the Irish in those days, they stuck together no matter what color suit they happened to wear.

Inside, White stood behind the bar chatting with Roland Shay, another of Schwartz's men, and your usual innocent bystander, a guy from the neighborhood named Karl Fischer. Tommy Krystal, the bouncer, stood just outside the front door, and in the back room, owner Moe Schwartz and bar manager Al Levy sat at a table playing cards.

If you're from anyplace else in the world, you might think it somewhat peculiar to have a notorious after-hours

FIGHTIN' IRISH: Harry "The Whiz" White won 20 prizefights and wasn't taking any nonsense the night troublemaking mobsters showed up at the Museum Grill.

joint located inside a museum, but people in Niagara Falls wouldn't bat an eyelash over such an arrangement.

After all, the Niagara Falls Museum itself was run by Saul Davis, a shady Canadian dealer of antiquities who'd built the fabulous five-story Gothic structure around the turn of the century to house a collection of Egyptian mummies, American Indian artifacts and two-headed farm animals he'd picked up for a song at an auction where other prospective buyers were discouraged both by his dubious reputation and by the size of the goons he brought with him to the sale.

So Saul was pals with Moe, and Moe was a friend of the Irish. Simple as that. Until about 4 o'clock that morning, when about a dozen Italian gentlemen led by Jimmy "The Horse Killer" Cini barged in, looking for trouble. Accompanied by Angelo Giambrone, Joe Ladota, Gerald Critelli, Nick Morrell and Jimmy Picorelli — among others — Cini walked in pushing the bouncer Tommy Krystal ahead of him.

Tommy was a tough guy, but nobody was that tough.

All of the men were associates of Falls mob chieftain Stefano Magaddino, whose Charles Distributing — later to become Power City Beverage — had a lock on the beer distribution business in Niagara Falls. When Moe Schwartz found he could buy beer cheaper someplace else, he told the Magaddinos they were no longer needed. So Cini and the boys dropped around that morning to have a "friendly discussion" about the matter and show Moe the error of his ways.

Things went bad quickly. According to later court testimony and police reports, Giambrone asked for a bottle of Chianti and was told by White there wasn't any. When White brought out a bottle of something else, one of the men threw it back at the ex-prizefighter, striking him in the head. White picked up a baseball bat and came around the bar. A melee ensued.

By the time the cops showed up at 5 a.m., the place was wrecked and eight men lay bleeding in the sawdust on the floor. Blue gunsmoke hung in the air below the white tin ceiling. Harry White was near death, a deep knife wound slashed across the width of his belly. Krystal had been similarly stabbed and wasn't expected to live. Shay also had a stab wound, apparently inflicted by an ice pick found at the scene.

Cini and Critelli had both been shot and were battered about the face and head, while Picorelli had a fractured skull and Ladota had been beaten and cut. The bystander, Karl Fischer, had been knocked cold when someone broke a chair over his head.

Police picked up five empty cartridge cases, flattened bullets that had missed their mark, a big pearl-handled jackknife with a long, open blade that had been sharpened like a razor, an ice pick, a couple of baseball bats and pieces of a .38 caliber revolver that had apparently been used as a bludgeon after its cylinder had been emptied.

All of the injured were rushed by ambulance to St. Mary's Hospital on Sixth Street. The lucky gambler Angelo Giambrone had escaped unscathed. Only Moe Schwartz and Al Levy were left to tell the story, and they weren't saying much.

By noon, Harry White had succumbed to his wounds, and the Irish cops now had the murder of an Irishman on their hands.

Harry's funeral was a grand affair; it was a shame he had to miss it. In Irish fashion, the body was laid out at the 1613 Weston Ave. home of his father, John J. White, and Mass was held the next morning at Sacred Heart. The papers said the funeral procession numbered more than 100 automobiles, including two carrying nothing but the expensive floral arrangements sent by Harry's friends and associates.

For his grieving wife, Dorothy, and the two fatherless boys, Harry Jr. and John, the gaudy display was cold comfort.

A grand jury was convened in Lockport to hear evidence in the case, while the various combatants found at the Museum Grill recovered from their injuries. The powerful and mobbed-up City Court Judge Angelo Scalzo announced that he would lead the defense team in the case after Cini, Ladota, Critelli, Picorelli and Morrell were charged by police with first-degree murder.

The men were members of an 11th Street crew known to police as the Cockroach Gang, reporters learned. The name of Stefano Magaddino was never publicly brought up in connection with the case.

The day after the White killing, Moe Schwartz was picked up and charged with selling booze after hours. The next thing he knew, Lee Beers, the county's liquor control officer, lifted his license. It was an outrage.

Schwartz pulled some strings at City Hall and in Lockport, however, and was back open for business that night.

Niagara County District Attorney Raymond A. Knowles betrayed the weakness of his case a few days later in a press interview. The prosecution had "seven different theories" about what had happened in the Museum Grill that morning, he said, and each was being explored.

Through Judge Scalzo, the Italian faction maintained that they had been set upon by the Irish unprovoked. There was no evidence of any premeditation or conspiracy on the part of the men, he said, and evidence would show that the person who stabbed Harry White and the others could not be identified by any of the witnesses.

The cops got a scare when they received word that a gang from Buffalo was on its way to the Falls with the intention of freeing the hospitalized Italians. Uniformed and plainclothes officers armed with machine guns, rifles and revolvers threw up a line of defense around St. Mary's, guarding every entrance and exit and lining the corridor where the wounded men lay.

Critelli, Cini and Picorelli were loaded into ambulances and whisked away under cover of darkness, accompanied by seven heavily armed officers.

The gang from Buffalo never showed up at the hospital, but the newspaper guys got a good story out of it, in any event.

Jury selection for the trial began on Dec. 3, less than six weeks after the killing of Harry White. Still, the headline in the old *Niagara Falls Gazette* complained, "Progress Is Slow." None of the jurors selected were from Niagara Falls, and none had an obviously Irish, Jewish or Italian surname. Several came from North Tonawanda, one from Lewiston, one from Royalton, one from Hartland, two from Cambria and one from Newfane.

In his opening remarks, District Attorney Knowles tossed a big-league curveball. He told the jurors they would hear of a "mysterious stranger," a man by the name of "Jimmy Sullivan."

Sullivan, he said, was the man who prevented the Italian gangsters from carrying out their intended wholesale slaughter that night in the Museum Grill.

"If it had not been for a mysterious individual named Jimmy Sullivan, who was in the grill on the morning of the murder, the five men under trial and seven others — indicted but unnamed — would have escaped and there would have been no witness left to tell what happened in the grill," Knowles said.

Fortunately, he added, Sullivan prevented this by shooting two of the men and driving the others out of the place after they had murdered White and left Krystal, Shay and the bystander Fischer down and wounded.

There was only one problem with the story Knowles told the jurors. Nobody knew who Sullivan was or where he might be found. He'd disappeared into the night like a comic book hero, leaving others to tell of his bold exploit.

It seemed a pretty slim reed on which to ask a jury of 12 grown men to condemn five other men to die in the electric chair at Sing Sing, but it was all Knowles had.

The prosecution's case was dealt another serious blow when several of its star witnesses, including Krystal — who testified from a stretcher — the bar manager Al Levy and the bystander Karl Fischer gave testimony that was significantly different from testimony they'd given to the grand jury just a couple of weeks earlier.

Under cross-examination, Krystal admitted he'd told the grand jury that Morrell had left the grill at least 10 minutes prior to the melee.

And Fischer now claimed that, at the first hint of trouble, he'd sought refuge in the men's room and didn't come out again until after it was all over. He testified further that he'd been so drunk that night to begin with, he didn't even remember entering the grill.

Scalzo demanded that the charges be dropped and his clients freed at once, which is probably exactly what would happen were the trial being held today. But it was 1934, the era of the Public Enemy. John Dillinger had been cut down unarmed in Chicago, and Pretty Boy Floyd died in a hail of bullets fired from behind as he ran through a plowed field in Ohio.

Niagara County Court Judge Alonzo G. Hinkley told Scalzo to sit down and shut up.

The prosecution rested its case, and the defense rested without calling a single witness. Scalzo told the jurors that the state had failed to prove any of the men on trial did anything wrong, much less planned and carried out the murder of Harry White.

Judge Hinkley took the unusual step of telling the jurors to forget about the first-degree murder charge and to consider a charge of manslaughter instead. The implication was clear: White was dead, and in all likelihood one of the defendants had killed him. Thus the jurors were relieved of having to think about complicated issues like conspiracy and premeditation. District Attorney Knowles was ecstatic.

Four of the defendants — Cini, Picorelli, Critelli and Ladota — were convicted on the manslaughter charge and sentenced to terms ranging from four to 12 years in Attica State Penitentiary. Charges against Morrell were dropped.

Harry White's widow said she feared retaliation from the Magaddino mob and fled with her sons to Pennsylvania. Following his service in World War II, Harry White Jr. returned to Niagara Falls to avenge his father's killing, but police got wind of his plans and he was picked up. After taking away the gun he had on him, the cops let him go with a warning never to come to Niagara Falls again.

Interestingly, Harry Jr. wound up in Albuquerque, N.M., where he raised a family. His son, Darren White, now serves as sheriff of Bernalillo County there.

"I realize my whole life has been shaped around a crime scene," he recently told the *Albuquerque Journal*. "I think about it every day I go to one."

Angelo Giambrone, who was present but never prosecuted in the White killing, continued on his merry way as a mobbed-up gambler here for the next 17 years. His luck ran out when he was unable to cover a series of bad bets he'd placed, and he was declared MIA by the police in 1951.

As for the Museum Grill, it continued to operate in the bowels of the Niagara Falls Museum, that imposing Gothic structure built by Saul Davis on a street known as Riverway, a picturesque strip overlooking the falls that was popular with the tourists.

That was right up until the state Parks Commission decided it could rake in millions of dollars each year by having its own parking lot. The entire street was taken, the museum and other buildings torn down, and an important part of Niagara Falls history was lost forever.

SUICIDE SEASON

By Mike Hudson

Memorial Day traditionally marks the beginning of the suicide season in Niagara Falls, but in recent years, the addition of the Seneca Niagara Casino has rather extended the period that a life-ending tumble over the mighty cataract seems like a viable option for many hopeless souls here.

Every year, between 20 and 25 people decide to end it all at Niagara Falls, which is second only to San Francisco's fabulous Golden Gate Bridge as the nation's top suicide destination. Perhaps unsurprisingly, most of the dead are locals, though the out-of-towners seem to grab the lion's share of the publicity.

Local historian Paul Gromosiak once wrote that 2,780 known suicides occurred here between 1856 and 1995, having compiled his grisly list from newspaper accounts of witnesses seeing someone jump or of bodies pulled out of the lower river. The actual number, he acknowledged at the time, is probably much higher, as many of the bodies are never recovered.

According to Gromosiak, the most popular day for someone to kill themselves at the falls is Monday, and the most popular time is 4 p.m. Traditionally, the gore starts picking up in April and increases as the weather gets warmer, culminating in a veritable orgy of death during the month of September.

An exhaustive study published in the *American Journal of Public Health* in 1991 showed that 59 percent of the jumpers are male and 41 percent female, which is highly unusual, in that female suicides account for just 24 percent of the total nationwide. Perhaps Oscar Wilde's famous quip about disappointed brides at Niagara Falls was truer than most people give it credit for.

The most suicidal women are 38 years of age, the study showed, while the men are most likely to be 39. Let's face it, nobody likes to celebrate their 40th birthday.

For years, the operators of the Maid of the Mist excursion boats enjoyed a lucrative sideline pulling bloated corpses out of the deep water directly below the falls, and that "Master Hero of Niagara,"

Red Hill Sr., launched a famous family dynasty performing similar work from the Canadian side of the river with his sons. Sadly, one of Hill's sons would die going over the falls in a contraption he made out of old inner tubes in 1951.

While most would-be suicides prefer the classic leap into the upper rapids near Prospect Point, others go with a spectacular 202-foot dive from the Rainbow Bridge. Other popular jumping-off points include various spots around Goat Island and the Three Sisters Islands, the Whirlpool Bridge and the rapids at Devil's Hole.

No one has ever survived a plunge over the American Falls, a fact noted by the famous mother-murderer and serial rapist Billy Shrubsall in the fake suicide note he left for authorities to find after he fled the United States to avoid imprisonment.

The Canadian Falls have proven to be marginally less fatal, in that 7-year-old Roger Woodward survived going over wearing a life preserver after a 1960 boating accident and, more recently, sad sack Kirk Jones stumbled over under mysterious circumstances in 2003.

At first, Jones said he did it as a stunt, later changing his story and alleging a botched suicide attempt when he discovered that fame and fortune were not to be his in the aftermath of his idiotic act.

The psychologists like to babble on about their own pet theories for people deciding to kill themselves here. They discuss the "mystique" of a falls suicide in terms of "committing one's body back to the force of nature," or the way in which the plunge somehow romanticizes their most desperate act.

Clearly, the shrinks haven't spent much time in the city of Niagara Falls. For local residents, living as they do in the shadow of the poisoned Love Canal, driving on streets so badly paved as to guarantee a snapped axle or at least a broken ball joint each year, laid off from their jobs and losing their unemployment checks at the casino, suicide can often seem like the best way out.

MYSTERY WOMAN TOOK SECRETS TO GRAVE

By Mike Hudson

Depending on who you talk to, Marie Jackson was either a lonely woman whose fantasies finally propelled her into the public eye, a mob moll in the classic tradition, or a government agent whose mission was to cause as much discomfort to the aging Don Stefano Magaddino as possible.

A decade has passed since her death in 1999, and gangland historians seem no closer to uncovering the truth about the mystery woman who brought the body of famed mob informant Joe Valachi to its final resting place at the Gate of Heaven Cemetery in Lewiston.

Valachi was a longtime drug dealer and sometime triggerman for the Genovese crime family in New York City whose life story became the subject of "The Valachi Papers" — a best-selling book by Peter Maas and a movie starring Charles Bronson — after he became a government informant in 1962.

Vito Genovese put out a $100,000 contract on Valachi that was never claimed, and the turncoat died of a heart attack at La Luna Federal Prison in El Paso, Texas, in 1971.

According to Maas, Marie Jackson never met Valachi, but began writing to him after seeing him on television testifying in 1963 during the Senate Rackets Committee hearings. Valachi had been greatly depressed at the time, he added.

"Miss Jackson's letters lifted his spirits," Maas told *The New York Times*. "When she would not write for a while, he would go back into depression and accuse the Justice Department of holding her letters."

A former Justice Department attorney who was in contact with Valachi at the time also said the two never met, though Jackson periodically sent Valachi money and gift boxes in addition to the letters.

One curious aspect of Valachi's testimony was that, for a guy from Brooklyn, he knew an awful lot about the Buffalo crime family and its boss, Stefano Magaddino. Much of what he told the senators had to do with Magaddino's involvement in the drug business and the horrific murder of drug runner Albert Agueci near Rochester in 1961.

That testimony stands out, because generally Valachi's knowledge of crime activity outside the five boroughs of New York City was quite limited.

Jackson herself gave an interview to Lou Michel of the *Buffalo News* in 1995 that directly contradicted the statements made by Maas and the Justice Department lawyer. Her version of the story goes a long way toward explaining Valachi's familiarity with the underworld of Niagara Falls and Buffalo.

The former Marie Murray was a Niagara Falls native and attended local schools before taking a job at the old Amberg's Men's Shop, where she met her future husband. The union was not a happy one, and was annulled by the Catholic Church after three years. He was Jewish and she was Catholic, and the religious difference was too much to overcome, she said.

Shortly after that, she said, she met Valachi at a house party thrown by a mutual friend in the Falls. He visited her regularly and paid her rent. They traveled extensively together, she said, and he often took her shopping in New York when she visited him there.

Valachi was arrested in 1960 for narcotics trafficking and sent to a federal prison in Georgia. In 1962, he beat another inmate to death with a lead pipe, mistaking the man for a mob hitman he believed was going to kill him. In order to escape the death penalty, he decided to rat out his former friends and associates.

Jackson took a job in an adult bookstore on 19th Street in order to make ends meet.

"It didn't bother me working there," she told Michel. "The money was good."

And she needed the money to pay for regular trips to Texas to visit her sweetheart.

While Valachi languished in a place where the mob could never get to him, Jackson lived unprotected in Niagara Falls, at the time a mafia stronghold of national repute.

"I told Joe I didn't fear many things," she said. "Joe raised the devil. He told everything. He said to hell with them, but if the mob would have gotten to him, they would have killed him."

RAT AT REST: Joe Valachi's grave at Gate of Heaven Cemetery.

Following Valachi's testimony, Jackson received a visit from some of the local wiseguys, she said.

"They said to me, 'We'll take care of things.' That was their way of speaking. But the mob left me alone. Joe had told me a lot of information, but I never said a word."

It was Valachi's death that put Jackson in the spotlight. His body lay unclaimed for two weeks by his estranged wife, Mildred, and son Donald before Jackson stepped forward to have it shipped to Lewiston. She paid $254 for his-and-hers gravestones, and another $115 for side-by-side burial plots at Gate of Heaven.

For her family, it was an uncomfortable time. Jackson's daughter, Karen Carlino, said her mother's relationship was a "deep, dark family secret."

"It was something that happened," she said. "It's in the past, and we're trying to forget about it."

Some in the underworld said at the time that bringing the rat to Lewiston, where Magaddino made his home, was a government setup designed solely to give the aging don a bad case of agita and perhaps hasten the onset of his own heart problems.

In any event, Jackson found herself labeled as "the mystery woman" in newspapers around the country, and the headlines continued as Valachi's will was read.

He'd left his entire estate to Jackson — who, mysteriously enough, was reportedly "vacationing in the Canary Islands" at the time the will was probated.

Royalties from the Maas book amounted to around $30,000 then, though Valachi had spent quite a bit of it, and Jackson was left with between $5,000 and $10,000, *The New York Times* reported.

But the next year, when the book became a hit movie grossing more than $20 million in worldwide release, Jackson's share of the royalties ballooned.

Though she wasn't mentioned in either the book or the film, she was besieged by writers seeking interviews or wanting to do her biography. She refused all such requests until four years before her death, when she sat down with Michel.

"I got a lot of money from the book," she told him.

CURIOUS CASE
OF STANFORD WHITE
By Mike Hudson

For some, the recent rescue of a historic home in the city's crumbling Echota subdivision marked the beginning of a new era of respect for the heritage of this most historic region.

But for others, the move toward resurrecting the largely abandoned neighborhood conjured up visions of one of the most lurid and sensational murders of the 20th century, a crime so shocking that a dozen books and at least two major motion pictures have been devoted to it.

For architect Stanford White, the 1890s were golden years. Based in New York City, he had designed and built the iconic Washington Square Arch there in 1889, and a series of lucrative commissions followed.

One of these was Echota in Niagara Falls, a planned community underwritten by the Niagara Falls Power Co. as an incentive for workers to locate near the Buffalo Avenue power station. Featuring its own community center, school, company store and public baths, Echota was dominated by beautiful, modern homes that came equipped with the latest in plumbing, electricity and appliances, set along wide and beautifully landscaped streets.

Located on what was then the edge of town, White's Echota development is often cited by historians as the nation's first planned community, the beginning of what would become the suburbanization of America.

In a city that even then had seen its share of improbable pipe dreams come to naught, Echota was a model of good planning, solid financing and the vision of a true genius — all turned into brick and mortar reality near the corner of Hyde Park Boulevard and Buffalo Avenue.

White grew into a figure of national prominence, and along with notoriety came wealth. While the combination has proven unfortunate for any number of individuals down through the centuries, for Stanford White it would be fatal.

DANGEROUS LIAISON: Comely chorine Evelyn Nesbit fell victim to wealthy architect Stanford White's lust for young flesh.

The acclaimed architect became what the newspapers of the day called "a notorious womanizer," specializing in young chorus girls from the Broadway stage, and rumors began to circulate about the curious nature of his sexual predilections. At least a portion of his riches were spent buying the silence of young women used and abused by White in pursuit of his insatiable lust.

In 1901, White became enamored with a ravishing 16-year-old named Evelyn Nesbit, who was then appearing in the chorus of "Floradora," said by theater buffs to be the first true Broadway musical. Although he was more than 30 years older than Evelyn, had a reputation as an abuser of women and was married to boot, the girl's pushy stage mother encouraged the relationship.

Young Evelyn was, after all, the family breadwinner.

When her mother left the city one week to take care of some family business in Pittsburgh, she basically entrusted Evelyn's care to the wealthy White. Much later, the girl would say that the architect got her high on morphine and champagne, and took pictures of her posing suggestively in a yellow silk kimono before deflowering her in a manner suggestive of what Freud would call sadomasochism and what the rest of us might think of as just plain creepy, to say the least.

It wasn't long before White began losing interest in his latest conquest, though he did help young Evelyn in her rise as both a Broadway star and an acclaimed artist's model.

She took up with John Barrymore Jr., a relationship opposed by both her mother and White on the grounds that the famous actor wasn't wealthy enough to take care of Evelyn in the style to which she'd become accustomed. She wouldn't be swayed, though, and continued seeing Barrymore on the sly.

White paid for her to have an abortion the first time she became pregnant by the actor and, the second time, paid for her to be sent away to a boarding school run by the mother of movie director Cecil B. DeMille, where it is believed she carried the baby to term before putting it up for adoption.

White's life continued pretty much as it had. He'd met and befriended the mysterious Serbian scientist Nikola Tesla while working in Niagara Falls, and Tesla commissioned him to build Wardenclyffe Tower, a huge radio transmission and electrical gen-erating station on Long Island, about which rumors have swirled since the United States government ordered it blown up in September of 1917.

Wardenclyffe Tower would be the last of White's designs to be built during his lifetime.

Following her breakup with Barrymore, the lovely Evelyn took up with Harry K. Thaw, the fabulously wealthy son of Pennsylvania coal mining and railroad baron Benjamin Thaw. An alcoholic and drug addict, Harry had been thrown out of numerous schools including Harvard University before drifting to New York and developing his own interest in showgirls.

He was particularly smitten by the pretty Evelyn, and asked her to marry him, an offer she initially refused due to the loss of her virginity to White. Thaw reportedly beat her with a dog whip in order to extract the lurid details of her sexual past but, despite his eccentricities, Evelyn finally gave in to Thaw's proposal and the two were married.

On a trip to New York in 1906, Thaw saw the celebrated White at Cafe Martin and then, accompanied by Evelyn, followed his man to the old Madison Square Garden, a building White had designed some 15 years earlier. Although it was a warm summer evening, Thaw wore a long overcoat to the show, and Evelyn commented on it.

The Garden's rooftop theater was hosting the sold-out premier of a racy new musical by Edgar Allan Woolf entitled "Mam'zelle

Champagne," and while White was simply there in search of another virginal chorus girl, Thaw had murder on his mind.

As the band and chorus broke into the play's signature number, "I Could Love A Million Girls," Thaw rose from his seat and approached White from behind.

"You ruined my life!" he cried, pulling a Colt .41 New Line revolver from under his coat.

White turned, and Thaw fired three shots into his face, killing the great man instantly.

Most of the people in the audience dismissed the episode as just another case of high society hijinks. But when White failed to get up, and the blood began to spread beneath the smartly shined shoes of the Smart Set, they realized the horrible truth.

Two trials followed. The first ended with a hung jury, while the second — in which Evelyn herself testified — resulted in a verdict of not guilty by reason of insanity.

Newspaper baron William Randolph Hearst sensationalized the retrial, and particularly Evelyn's testimony, on the front pages of newspapers across the country. The second trial became, in popular parlance, "The Trial of the Century."

Evelyn said she was raped by White, and spun seedy yarns about a red velvet swing the architect had installed in his spacious tower apartment. Thaw said he'd suffered "a brainstorm" that night at the Garden to prop up the contention that he was not responsible for his act.

He was committed to a mental institution, escaped, was recaptured and was finally freed in 1915. The next year, he was arrested for sexually assaulting and horsewhipping teenager Fred B. Gump Jr. and sent to another mental hospital, where he spent seven years. He died in Miami at the age of 76 in 1941, leaving what remained of his fortune — around $10,000 — to Evelyn, whom he hadn't seen in many years.

After the second trial, Evelyn had an unsuccessful career in vaudeville, attempted suicide several times, and renewed her love affairs with booze and dope. In 1955, she worked as a technical adviser on the film "The Girl in the Red Velvet Swing," an account of the events leading up to White's murder. A young Joan Collins played her in the film, while White was played by Ray Milland.

Later, in the film version of E.L. Doctorow's novel "Ragtime," White was played by the author Norman Mailer, whose own libertine lifestyle has been well documented.

As is often the case in Niagara Falls, what is seen on the surface can reveal an entirely different and frequently disturbing story lurking underneath.

Take the crumbling Echota neighborhood at the corner of Hyde Park Boulevard and Buffalo Avenue, for example.

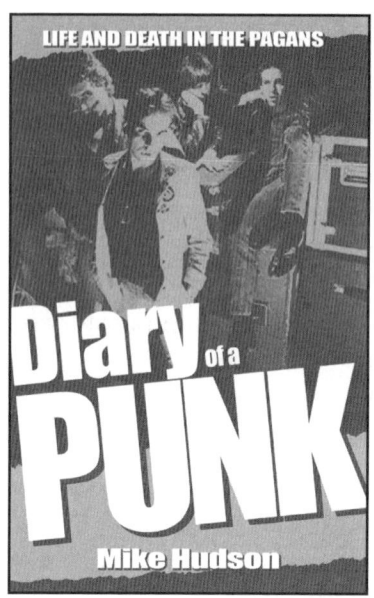

Thirty years ago, Mike Hudson was at the forefront of the groundbreaking punk rock movement with Cleveland's now-legendary Pagans. Sometimes poetic, sometimes angry, *Diary of a Punk* tells Mike's story of those years and what came after in unique and uncompromising style. He paints a stark insider's portrait of a life lived outside society's boundaries.

ISBN 978-0-9797693-1-3
160 pages, illustrated
$19.95

Praise for DIARY OF A PUNK ...

"A down-and-dirty tell-all and a nice zoom into a musical tale every bit as involving as 'England's Dreaming' or 'Please Kill Me.' Hudson is nothing if not gutsy; clearly, he's still a punk at heart. I can honestly give 'Diary of a Punk' perhaps the finest praise one can heap upon a music bio:
it made me want to listen to his band. Loudly. Right now."
- Christopher Schobert, Buffalo Spree

"He carves out words like a butcher carves a steak. Sometimes there's blood on the chopping block."
- George Sample, Corry (Pa.) Journal

"Riveting, rattling and detailed ... full of death-defying tales, angry Cleveland brio and self-inflected disasters. It's truly as punk as the band ever was."
- Ira Robbins, Trouser Press

Don Stefano Magaddino murdered his way from the sleepy Sicilian village of Castellamare del Golfo to the mean streets of Brooklyn before heading to Western New York and seizing control of the notorious Buffalo mob. Based on interviews with underworld and law enforcement sources, Mike Hudson's *Mob Boss* is sure to take its place among the classics of mafia literature!

ISBN 978-0-615-23073-3
120 pages, illustrated
$19.95

ABOUT THE AUTHOR

Mike Hudson is a writer and musician whose byline has appeared in the *Irish Echo, Hustler, Master Detective, FATE, Field & Stream, Lost Treasure, Cle*, the Associated Press, *Hey Daddy-O* and many other publications. He has worked for newspapers in Ohio, Pennsylvania and New York, and currently edits the *Niagara Falls Reporter*.

He was also the founder and lead singer of the seminal American punk rock group the Pagans, whose 11 albums continue to sell more than two decades after the band broke up.

In addition to *Niagara Falls Confidential*, he is the author of *Mob Boss*, a full-length biography of New York mafia kingpin Stefano Magaddino, and *Diary of a Punk*, a memoir of his life in music. The British Overground label released a spoken word recording of several of his short stories, *All the Wrong People Are Dying*, in 1998.

Hudson lives in Niagara Falls with his wife and collaborator Rebecca Hudson and their five cats.